50 knitted gifts
for year-round giving

made especially
for you

50 knitted gifts

for year-round giving

◆ DESIGNS FOR EVERY
SEASON AND OCCASION
FEATURING UNIVERSAL YARN
DELUXE WORSTED

THE EDITORS OF SIXTH&SPRING BOOKS

sixth&spring
books
NEW YORK

sixth&spring
books

161 Avenue of the Americas
New York, NY 10013
SIXTHANDSPRINGBOOKS.COM

EDITORIAL DIRECTOR
JOY AQUILINO

DEVELOPMENTAL EDITOR
LISA SILVERMAN

ART DIRECTOR
DIANE LAMPHRON

YARN EDITOR
CHRISTINA BEHNKE

EDITORIAL/ART
ASSISTANT
JOHANNA LEVY

GRAPHIC DESIGNER
DEBORAH GRISORIO

INSTRUCTIONS EDITORS
BARBARA KHOURI
RACHEL MAURER
STEPHANIE MRSE
JUDY SLOAN

PROOFREADER
KRISTIN JONES

TECHNICAL
ILLUSTRATOR
ULI MONCH

FASHION STYLIST
KHALIAH JONES

PHOTOGRAPHER
JACK DEUTSCH

VICE PRESIDENT
TRISHA MALCOLM

PUBLISHER
CARRIE KILMER

PRODUCTION
MANAGER
DAVID JOINNIDES

PRESIDENT
ART JOINNIDES

CHAIRMAN
JAY STEIN

Library of Congress Cataloging-in-Publication Data is available from the Library of Congress.

ISBN: 978-1-936096-56-5

MANUFACTURED IN CHINA

1 3 5 7 9 10 8 6 4 2

First Edition

UNIVERSAL YARN
universalyarn.com

Contents

Preface

In 2005, Hal Ozbelli founded Universal Yarn with the goal of offering high-quality hand-knitting yarns in a broad array of colors, softness, and textures. With an eye toward creating a company that would serve every category of local yarn stores, Universal Yarn took its first steps as a knowledgeable source for novelty, fur, and fantasy yarns, providing service to shops throughout the United States.

As knitters' preferences turned "back to basics," Universal expanded its offerings to develop two yarn store stand-bys: The Classic Collection, a line of machine-washable and -dryable wool-acrylic blended yarns, and The Deluxe Collection, a line of soft, 100% wool ideal for textured, colorwork, and felting projects. Working directly with technicians and color experts at the mill, Universal Yarn developed and released Deluxe Worsted and Chunky. With felting a growing trend among knitters, Universal paid close attention to the color and treatment of the yarn, ensuring that all colors—even the white—would felt thoroughly and easily.

After the first release of the Deluxe Collection of wools, Universal Yarn grew rapidly by adding Long Print, a line of self-striping colors; Instant Print, a collection of patterning colors; and later an expansive line of natural, heathered, tweed, and solid colors, rounding out the palette to more than 200 colors. Universal is also expanding its offerings to include a palette of nearly fifty superwash solids in the same reliable worsted weight.

Holiday gift-giving continues to be a major source of satisfaction for knitters. In this volume, Universal has partnered with expert designers to create fifty ways to celebrate the holidays year-round with knitted gifts. Whether you're knitting a gift for a friend or family member, or a special gift for yourself, you'll find something for every recipient in this inspired collection.

Looking ahead, Universal Yarn is committed to serving knitters and local yarn communities everywhere by providing a wide range of price-conscious, quality yarns from basic to fancy to trend-driven styles, and more fantastic books like this collection from our friends at Sixth&Spring.

Michael del Vecchio
Executive Creative Director
Universal Yarn

New Year's Eve Necklace

A self-patterning yarn makes it easy to create this colorful necklace that alternates knitted balls with beads. Wear it on New Year's, or dress it down the rest of the year.

◆

Designed by Tanis Gray

KNITTED MEASUREMENTS
Finished length approx 40"/102cm

MATERIALS
■ 1 3½oz/100g skein (each approx 219yds/200m) Universal Yarn *Deluxe Worsted Instant Print* (100% wool) in #120-03

■ Contrasting scrap yarn for provisional cast-on

■ One set (4) size 5 (3.75mm) double-pointed needles (dpns) OR SIZE TO OBTAIN GAUGE

■ Size F/5 (3.75mm) crochet hook

■ 1½ yd/1.5m nylon fishing line

■ Sharp tapestry needle

■ 35 1"/2.5cm Styrofoam balls

■ 35 blue, white-lined 9mm glass pony beads

GAUGE
22 sts and 30 rows = 4"/10cm over St st using size 5 (3.75mm) needles.
TAKE TIME TO CHECK GAUGE.

KNITTED BALLS (MAKE 35)
Using provisional cast-on, cast on 16 sts and distribute over 3 dpns. Join to work in rnds, taking care not to twist sts. Place marker for end of rnd. Work in desired pattern and St st for 10 rnds. Break yarn, leaving a 10"/25cm tail. Thread tail through sts and pull tight. Knot securely and trim tail. Insert Styrofoam ball, with knot on WS of ball. Remove provisional cast-on, place sts on one dpn. Thread tail through sts and pull tight. Knot securely and trim tail, with knot on WS of ball.

FINISHING
With nylon fishing line on tapestry needle, insert from top to bottom through center of each ball and string in desired order, alternating one ball with one bead. Knot nylon line securely and trim ends. 🎀

JANUARY
1

Champagne Toast Wine Cozy

Make the hostess gift for a New Year's party even more memorable by wrapping it in this collared cozy, with a striking cable panel in the center.

◆

Designed by Anastasia Blaes

SIZE
To fit 750ml bottle.

KNITTED MEASUREMENTS
Height 11"/28cm
Circumference 10"/25.5cm

MATERIALS
■ 1 3½oz/100g skein (each approx 220yd/201m) of Universal Yarn *Deluxe Worsted* (100% wool) in #71662 turquoise

■ One set (4) size 6 (4mm) double-pointed needles, OR SIZE TO OBTAIN GAUGE

■ Size 6 (4mm) circular needle, 24" long

■ Cable needle (cn)

■ Stitch marker

GAUGES
20 sts and 28 rows = 4"/10cm over St st using size 6 (4mm) needles.
32 sts and 36 rows = 4"/10cm over pat st (unstretched) using size 6 (4mm) needles.
TAKE TIME TO CHECK GAUGES.

STITCH GLOSSARY
6-st RC Sl 3 sts to cn and hold to *back*, k3, k3 from cn.
6-st LC Sl 3 sts to cn and hold to *front*, k3, k3, from cn.

COZY
Cast on 66 sts. Divide sts onto 3 dpns and join to work in the rnd, being careful not to twist sts. Pm for beg of rnd.
Rnds 1 and 2 *K1, p2, k12, p2, [k1, p1] 8 times; rep from * once more.
Rnd 3 *K1, p2, 6-st RC, 6-st LC, p2, [k1, p1] 8 times; rep from * once more.
Rnds 4–10 Rep rnd 1.
Rnd 11 *K1, p2, 6-st LC, 6-st RC, p2, [k1, p1] 8 times; rep from * once more.
Rnds 12–16 Rep rnd 1.
Rep rnds 3–16, four times more (measures approx 8"/20.5cm from beg), then work rnds 1 and 2.

COLLAR
Set-up rnd K1, p2, k6, bind off 4 sts, k1, p2tog, [k1, p1] 8 times, k1, p2tog, ssk, p1, k1, p1, ssk, p1, k1, p1, k2tog, p2tog, [k1, p1] 8 times, sm, k1, p2tog, k6—55 sts. Turn. You will now be working the collar back and forth in rows.
Row 1 (WS) Bind off 4 sts, p1, *k1, p1; rep from * to last st, end k1—51 sts.
Sl first st of each row purlwise for selvedge and cont as established, working k1, p1 rib back and forth until collar measures approx 3"/7.5cm and entire cozy measures 11"/28cm from beg. Bind off.
Weave in all ends. 🎀

Midnight Kiss Capelet

Complement a shoulder-baring gown on New Year's Eve with a fancy and feminine capelet, featuring a uniquely beautiful scalloped color pattern.

Designed by Robyn M. Schrager

SIZE
One size (adult)

KNITTED MEASUREMENTS
Height approx 16"/42cm
Neck edge approx 26"/66cm
Bottom edge approx 60"/152.5cm

MATERIALS
■ 2 3½oz/100g skeins (each approx 220yd/201m) Universal Yarn *Deluxe Worsted* (100% wool) in #12291 petit pink (MC)

■ 1 skein in #12172 dark crystal (CC)

■ Size 7 (4.5mm) circular needle, 32"/81cm long, OR SIZE TO OBTAIN GAUGE

■ Stitch markers

■ 1 frog or clasp closure

GAUGES
18 sts and 28 rows = 4"/10cm over pat using size 7 (4.5mm) needles.
18 sts and 30 rows = 4"/10cm over St st using size 7 (4.5mm) needles.
TAKE TIME TO CHECK GAUGES.

NOTES
1) The capelet is worked from the bottom up in 2 contrasting colors. Do not cut yarn between color changes, but twist the 2 strands at the beg of every RS row to carry the unused yarn up the side. Decreases are worked in the garter st rows transitioning from swag to scallop sections.
2) The last st of every row is sl purlwise wyif.

STITCH GLOSSARY
E (edge st) Sl last st of row purlwise wyif.
MS Insert right needle under 2 loose strands of CC, into next MC st, and knit all 3 tog.

SCALLOP PATTERN
(multiple of 11 sts plus 2)
Row 1 (RS) K1 tbl, *k2tog, k2, [kf&b] twice, k3, k2tog tbl; rep from * to last st, E.
Row 2 K1 tbl, purl to last st, E.
Rep rows 1 and 2 twice more for scallop pat.

MOSAIC SWAG PATTERN
(multiple of 6 sts plus 7)
Row 1 (RS) With MC, k1 tbl, knit to last st, E.
Row 2 (WS) K1 tbl, p to last st, E. Change to CC.
Row 3 K1 tbl, p4, *sl3 wyif, p3; rep from * to last 2 sts, p1, E.
Row 4 K1 tbl, k4, *sl3 wyib, k3; rep from * to last 2 sts, k1, E. Change to MC.
Row 5 Rep row 1.

Row 6 Rep row 2.
Row 7 K1 tbl, k5, *MS, k5; rep from * to last st, E.
Row 8 Rep row 2. Change to CC.
Row 9 K1 tbl, p1, *sl3 wyif, p3; rep from * to last 5 sts, sl 3 wyif, p1, E.
Row 10 K1 tbl, k1, *sl3 wyib, k3; rep from * to last 5 sts, sl3 wyib, k1, E. Change to MC.
Row 11 Rep row 1.
Row 12 Rep row 2.
Row 13 K1 tbl, k2, *MS, k5; rep from * to last 4 sts, MS, k2, E.
Row 14 Rep row 2.
Rep rows 3–14 for mosaic swag pat.

CAPELET
With CC, cast on 222 sts.
Rows 1–3 K1 tbl, knit to last st, E. Switch to MC.
Rows 4–5 Knit to last st, E.
Work scallop pat for 6 rows.
Next row K1 tbl, k110, kf&b, knit to last st, E—223 sts.
Next row K1 tbl, purl to last st, E. Change to CC.
Beg mosaic swag pat, work rows 3–14 four times for a total of 8 swag rows. Change to CC.
Next row K1 tbl, knit to last st, E.
Next row K1 tbl, k2tog, k2, (k2tog, k3) 43 times, k2tog, E. Switch to MC—178 sts.
Next 2 rows K1 tbl, knit to last st, E.
Work scallop pat for 6 rows.

Next row (RS) K1 tbl, k88, kf&b, knit to last st, E—175 sts.

Next row K1 tbl, purl to last st, E. Change to CC.

Work mosaic swag pat, working rows 3–14 twice for a total of 4 swag rows. Change to CC.

Next row (RS) K1 tbl, knit to last st, E.

Next row K1 tbl, k1, [k2tog, k3] twice, [k2tog, k4] 25 times, [k2tog, k3] twice, k2tog, E. Change to MC—145 sts.

Next 2 rows K1 tbl, knit to last st, E. Work scallop pat for 6 rows.

Next row (RS) K1 tbl, knit to last st, E.

Next row K1 tbl, [p2tog, p2] twice, [p2tog, p3] 25 times, [p2tog, p2] twice, p2tog, E. Change to CC—115 sts.

Work mosaic swag pat, working rows 3–14 once for a total of two swag rows. Change to CC.

Next row (RS) K1 tbl, knit to last st, E.

Next row K1 tbl, k17, k2tog, k36, k2tog, k37, k2tog, k17, E. Change to MC—112 sts.

Next 2 rows K1 tbl, knit to last st, E. Work scallop pat for 6 rows.

Next 5 rows With CC, k1 tbl, knit to last st, E.

Bind off loosely.

I-CORD EDGING

With WS facing, and using MC, beg at the first MC row, pick up and k 1 st in each edge st, ending with the last MC row. Cast on 3 sts.

Row 1 K2, k2tog tbl. Sl these sts back onto left needle.

Rep until all picked-up stitches are gone. Bind off 3 sts.

Repeat for opposite front edge.

FINISHING

Weave in ends. Block lightly, keeping the swags slightly raised above the MC, as desired. Attach clasp. ✿

Auld Lang Syne Mitts

Keep your hands warm at midnight and still show off that holiday manicure. These fingerless mitts feature a fun and easy cable eyelet pattern with garter stitch trim.

Designed by Triona Murphy

SIZES
Adult Small/Medium (Large/X-Large)

KNITTED MEASUREMENTS
Palm circumference 7½"/19cm (8½"/21.5cm)
Length from edge to top of mitt 8½"/21.5cm

MATERIALS
■ 1 (1) 3½oz/100g skein (each approx 220yd/201m) of Universal Yarn *Deluxe Worsted* (100% wool) in #12267 dolphin

■ One set (5) each sizes 6 (4mm) and 7 (4.5mm) double-pointed needles (dpns) OR SIZE TO OBTAIN GAUGE

■ Stitch markers

■ Tapestry needle

■ Cable needle (cn)

■ Waste yarn

GAUGE
18 sts and 26 rows = 4" in St st on larger needles.
TAKE TIME TO CHECK GAUGE.

NOTES
1) The cable pattern is mirrored on each mitt, so the cable motif starts on a different round for each. The thumb placement is also different on the right and left mitts. Make sure to read the instructions carefully.

2) For a longer cuff, work an extra full repeat of the wavy cable pattern before beginning the thumb gusset.

STITCH GLOSSARY
2-st RC Sl next st to cn and hold to *back*, k2, k1 from cn.
2-st LC Sl next 2 sts to cn and hold to *front*, k1, k2 from cn.

WAVY CABLE PATTERN
(over 12 sts)
Rnd 1 and all odd-numbered rnds Knit.
Rnd 2 [K2tog, yo] 3 times, k6.
Rnd 4 K1, [k2tog, yo] twice, k1, 2-st RC, k3.
Rnd 6 K2, k2tog, yo, k1, 2-st RC, k4.
Rnd 8 K4, 2-st RC, k1, yo, ssk, k2.
Rnd 10 K3, 2-st RC, k1, [yo, ssk] twice, k1.
Rnd 12 K6, [yo, ssk] 3 times.
Rnd 14 K3, 2-st LC, k1, [yo, ssk] twice, k1.
Rnd 16 K4, 2-st LC, k1, yo, ssk, k2.
Rnd 18 K2, k2tog, yo, k1, 2-st LC, k4.
Rnd 20 K1, [k2tog, yo] twice, k1, 2-st LC, k3.
Rep rnds 1–20 for wavy cable pat.

RIGHT MITT
CUFF
With smaller dpns, cast on 32 (36) sts. Arrange sts as foll: 10 (12) sts on needle 1, 12 sts on needle 2, 10 (12) sts on needle 3. Pm and join to work in the rnd.
Rnd 1 Knit.
Rnd 2 Purl. Rep these 2 rnds until cuff measures 1" from cast-on edge, ending with rnd 2. Switch to larger dpns.

BEG CABLE PAT
Rnd 1 Knit across sts on ndl 1, work rnd 1 of wavy cable pat across 12 sts on needle 2, knit to end.
Cont in pat, knitting all sts on needle 1 and 3, and working needle 2 in cable pat for 19 more rnds. Work should measure approx 4" from cast-on edge.

THUMB GUSSET
Note Cont to work rnds 1–20 of wavy cable pat as est while following these instructions.
Rnd 1 Work across needle 1 and 2 in pat, k2, pm, M1R, k1, M1L, pm, knit to end—2 sts inc'd.
Rnd 2 Work even in pat.
Rnd 3 Work across needle 1 and 2 in pat, k2, sl m, M1R, knit to m, M1L, sl m, knit to end—2 sts inc'd.
Rep rnds 2 and 3 for 3 (4) times more—11 (13) thumb sts, 42 (48) sts total. Rep rnd 2 once more.
Next rnd Work in pat to m. Remove m, sl next 11 (13) sts to waste yarn, rem m, cast on 4 sts across the gap using the backward loop method, knit to end—35 (39) sts.

Next rnd Work across needles 1 and 2 in pat, k1, ssk, k2, k2tog, k to end—33 (37) sts rem.

PALM
Work even in pat as set, ending with the next rnd 3 of wavy cable pat, or until mitt measures approx 7½" from cast-on edge.

UPPER TRIM
Switch to smaller dpns.
Rnd 1 Knit.
Rnd 2 Purl.
Rep rnds 1 and 2 until mitt measures 8½" from cast-on. Bind off all sts loosely knitwise.

THUMB
Place 11 (13) held sts on larger dpns. Attach yarn to beg of needle 1.
Set-up rnd Knit to gap, pick up and knit 4, pm and join—15 (17) sts.
Next rnd Knit to last 4 sts, ssk, k2tog—13 (15) sts rem. Knit 2 rnds even.

THUMB TRIM
Switch to smaller dpns.
Rnd 1 Knit.
Rnd 2 Purl.
Rep rnds 1 and 2 until thumb trim measures 1". Bind off all sts loosely knitwise.

LEFT MITT
Work as for right mitt to begin of cable pat.
Rnd 1 Knit across sts on needle 1, work rnd 11 of wavy cable pat across 12 sts on needle 2, knit to end. Cont in pat, knitting all sts on needles 1 and 3, and working needle 2 in cable pat for 19 more rnds. Work should measure approx 4" from cast-on edge.

THUMB GUSSET
Note Cont to work rnds 1–20 of wavy cable pat as set while following these instructions.
Rnd 1 K7 (9), pm, M1R, k1, M1L, pm, k2, work across needles 1 and 2 in pat—2 sts inc'd.
Rnd 2 Work even in pat.
Rnd 3 Knit to m, sl m, M1R, knit to m, M1L, sl m, work in pat to end—2 sts inc'd.
Rep rnds 2 and 3 for 3 (4) times more—11 (13) thumb sts, 42 (48) sts total. Rep rnd 2 once more.
Next rnd Knit to m, remove m, sl next 11 (13) sts to waste yarn, remove m, cast on 4 sts across gap using backward loop method, work in pat to end—35 (39) sts.
Next rnd Knit to 7 sts before end of needle 1, ssk, k2, k2tog, k1, work in pat to end—33 (37) sts rem.

PALM
Work even in pat as set, ending with the next rnd 13 of wavy cable pat, or until mitt measures approx 7½" from cast-on edge. Complete as for right mitt.

FINISHING
Weave in ends and block lightly. 🎀

Wishing you a very Happy New Year!

Happy Couple Cup Snuggies

Keep your hands comfy with these heart-adorned cozies while you share a cup of warmth with your sweetheart.

Designed by Cheryl Murray

KNITTED MEASUREMENTS
Height 3½"/9cm
Bottom circumference 7½"/19cm
Top circumference 8½"/21.5cm

MATERIALS
■ 1 3½oz/100g skein (each 220yd/201m) Universal Yarn *Deluxe Worsted* (100% wool) each in #12294 real red (A) and #12291 petit pink (B)

■ One set (5) size 7 (4.5mm) double-pointed needles (dpns) OR SIZE TO OBTAIN GAUGE

■ Stitch markers

GAUGE
20 sts and 28 rows = 4"/10cm over St st in the rnd using size 7 (4.5mm) needles.
TAKE TIME TO CHECK GAUGE.

NOTES
1) Yarn quantity is sufficient to make several sleeves. For two versions shown, reverse colors A and B.
2) Sleeve is designed to fit a 16oz disposable coffee cup.

SLEEVES
With A, cast on 36 sts using long-tail method. Divide evenly on dpns. Join in the rnd, being careful not to twist. Pm for beg of rnd.
Rnds 1–23 Work rnds 1–23 of chart, working each row twice for each rnd. Work inc on rnds 7 and 17 as indicated on the chart—44 sts.
Bind off purlwise.

FINISHING
Weave in ends. Block gently. ✄

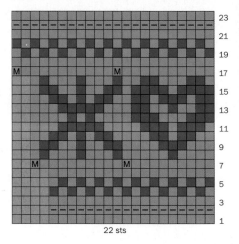

22 sts

COLOR AND STITCH KEY
■ Knit with A
■ Knit with B
– Purl with B
M M1 with B
□ No stitch

Valentine's Hot Water Bottle Cozy

What's more soothing than a hot water bottle?
One with a soft knitted cover that closes with a buttoned flap.

Designed by Jacqueline van Dillen

KNITTED MEASUREMENTS
Width approx 8½"/21.5cm
Length approx 10¾"/27.5cm
(excluding neck)

MATERIALS
■ 1 3½oz/100g skein (each approx 220yd/201m) of Universal Yarn *Deluxe Worsted* (100% wool) each in #12236 violet glow (MC) and #12287 cerise (CC)

■ One pair size 7 (4.5mm) needles OR SIZE TO OBTAIN GAUGE

■ 2 ½" buttons

GAUGE
18 sts and 24 rows = 4"/10cm over St st using size 7 (4.5mm) needles.
TAKE TIME TO CHECK GAUGE.

K1, P1 RIB
(over odd number of sts)
Row 1 *K1, p1, rep from * to last st, k1.
Row 2 *P1, k1, rep from * to last st, p1.
Rep rows 1 and 2 for k1, p1 rib.

FRONT
With MC, cast on 25 sts. Working in St st, beg with RS row, inc 1 st at beg of next 4 rows—29 sts.
Row 5 (RS) K1, M1, k7, cast off 2 sts for buttonhole, k10, cast off 2 sts for buttonhole, k8.
Row 6 (WS) P1, M1, p7, cast on 2 sts, p10, cast on 2 sts, p8.
Cont in St st, inc 1 st at beg of next 15 rows—45 sts.
*Work straight for 2¼"/4cm, then work 6 rows CC and 6 rows MC.

Work chart in St st over center 25 sts, then continue in MC.
When the total body length is 20"/51cm, decrease 1 st at end of next 10 rows—35 sts.
Bind off 9 sts at beg of next 2 rows—17sts.
Work in k1, p1 rib for 4¾"/12cm.
Bind off in rib.

BACK
With MC, cast on 35 sts. Inc 1 st at beg of next 10 rows—45 sts.
Work as given for front from *.

FINISHING
Weave in ends. Sew sides together, reversing seam for foldover of neck.
Leave bottom open.
Sew buttons onto bottom of back to correspond with buttonholes on front flap.
Block lightly to measurements. 🪁

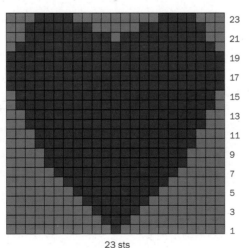

23 sts

23 21 19 17 15 13 11 9 7 5 3 1

COLOR AND STITCH KEY
■ K on RS, p on WS in MC
■ P on RS, k on WS in CC

Sweetheart Lacy Cowl

This pretty cowl with a heart-shaped lace pattern is the perfect accessory for a romantic midwinter date.

Designed by Cheryl Murray

KNITTED MEASUREMENTS
Circumference approx 22"/56cm
Height approx 9"/23cm

MATERIALS
■ 1 3 ½oz/100g skein (each approx 220yd/201m) of Universal Yarn *Deluxe Worsted* (100% wool) in #12289 blushing bride

■ Size 8 (5mm) circular needle, 16"/41cm long, OR SIZE TO OBTAIN GAUGE

■ Stitch marker

GAUGE
18 sts and 32 rows = 4"/10cm over St st on size 8 (5mm) needles.
TAKE TIME TO CHECK GAUGE.

NOTE
Cowl body is worked in the round. Edging is worked flat.

COWL
Cast on 100 sts. Join in the rnd, being careful not to twist sts, pm for beg of rnd.
Set-up rnd [K25, pm] three times, k25.

BEG CHART 1
Beg with rnd 1, rep chart four times around for each rnd.
Work rnds 1–18 three times.
Rnd 55 Purl.
Rnd 56 Knit.
Bind off purlwise.

EDGING
Cast on 6 sts. Work rows 1–8 of chart 2. Rep until edging is long enough to go around entire lower edge of cowl, ending with row 8 of chart. Bind off all sts.

FINISHING
Join cast-on edge of edging to bind-off edge. Placing edging and body of cowl side by side, sew lefthand side of edging to cast-on edge of cowl.
Weave in ends. Block to measurements.

CHART 2

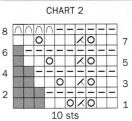

10 sts

CHART 1

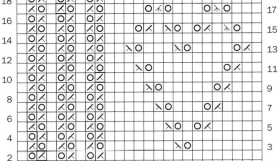

25 sts

STITCH KEY
□ K on RS, p on WS
– P on RS, k on WS
⟋ K2tog
⟍ Ssk
⟓ Sssk
⟎ K3tog
▨ No stitch
○ Yo (yarn over)
⌒ Bind off

St. Patrick's Day Beret

Irish eyes will smile when they spot the cleverly constructed
Celtic motif on this multi-textured beret.

◆

Designed by Andrea Babb

SIZE
One size (adult)

KNITTED MEASUREMENTS
Brim circumference 19" (unstretched)

MATERIALS
■ 2 3½oz/100g skeins (each approx 220yd/201m) of Universal Yarn *Deluxe Worsted* (100% wool) in #12507 shamrock heather

■ One set size 6 (4mm) needles OR SIZE TO OBTAIN GAUGE

■ Size 6 (4mm) circular needle, 24"/60cm long

■ Two (2) size 6 (4mm) double-pointed needles (dpns)

■ Cable needle (cn)

■ Stitch holder

GAUGE
20 sts and 36 rows = 4"/10cm in seed stitch using size 6 (4mm) needles.
TAKE TIME TO CHECK GAUGE.

STITCH GLOSSARY
kfb Knit in front and back of st.
5-st bobble K into front and back of st 5 times. Turn, p5. Turn, k5. Turn, p2tog, p1, p2tog. Turn, SK2P.
4-st RC Slip 2 sts to cn and hold in *back*, k2, k2 from cn.
4-st LC Slip 2 sts to cn and hold in *front*, k2, k2 from cn.

I-CORD
With dpns, cast on 3 sts. *K3 sts, do not turn, but slide sts to other end of needle. Rep from * until cord measures desired length.

SEED STITCH
(over odd number of sts)
Row 1 (RS) K1, *p1, k1; rep from * to end.
Row 2 (WS) P the knit sts, k the purl sts.
Repeat row 2 for seed st.

RIGHT CABLE
(over 4 sts)
Row 1 (RS) Work 4-st RC.
Row 2 (WS) Purl.
Row 3 Knit.
Row 4 Purl.
Rep rows 1–4 for right cable.

LEFT CABLE
(over 4 sts)
Row 1 (RS) Work 4-st LC.
Row 2 (WS) Purl.
Row 3 Knit.
Row 4 Purl.
Rep rows 1–4 for left cable.

BOBBLE PATTERN
Row 1 P1, k1, p2, work bobble, p2, k2.
Rows 2, 4, and 6 P2, k5, p1, k1.
Rows 3, 5, and 7 P1, k1, p5, k2.
Row 8 P2, k5, p1, k1.
Rep rows 1–8 for bobble pat.

TOP
With straight needles, cast on 15 sts.
Row 1 (RS) Kfb, *k1, p1; rep from * to last 2 sts, k1, kfb—17 sts.
Row 2 (WS) Kfb, work in seed st as est to last 2 sts, k1, kfb—19 sts.
Working incs into seed st, inc 1 st each side as est every row 10 times more—39 sts. Inc 1 st each side every RS row 1 time, every 4th row 3 times, every 6th row 2 times, then every 4th row 1 time—53 sts. Work even in seed st for 15 rows.
Next (dec) row (RS) K2tog, work in seed st to last 2 sts, ssk. Rep dec row every 4th row 1 time, every 6th row 2 times, every 4th row 3 times, then every 2nd row 1 time—37 sts.
Next (dec) row (WS) P2tog, work in seed st to last 2 sts, p2tog tbl. Dec 1 st each side as est every row 10 times more—15 sts. Bind off.

CROWN
With circular needle, cast on 163 sts. Do *not* join to work in rnd—circular needle is used to accommodate large number of sts.
Set-up row (WS) [K1, p1] 5 times, p4,

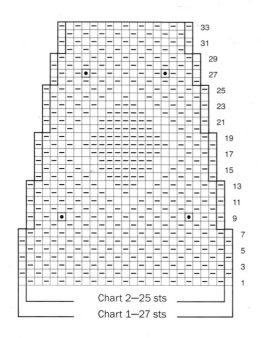

Chart 2—25 sts
Chart 1—27 sts

STITCH KEY

☐ K on RS, p on WS

⊟ P on RS, k on WS

⊡ Make bobble

NOTE: Work full chart (27 sts, decreasing to 17) for chart 1. For chart 2, work the area within the red lines (2 fewer stitches in each repeat).

[k1, p1] 10 times, k1, p4, [p1, k1] 12 times, p1, p4, [k1, p1] 13 times, k1, p4, [p1, k1] 12 times, p1, p4, [k1, p1] 10 times, k1, p4, [p1, k1] 5 times.
Row 1 (RS) Work in seed st over 10 sts, work row 1 of right cable, work seed st over 21 sts, work row 1 of right cable, work row 1 of chart 2 over next 25 sts, work row 1 of right cable, work row 1 of chart 1 over next 27 sts, work row 1 of left cable, work row 1 of chart 2 over next 25 sts, work row 1 of left cable, work seed st over next 21 sts, work row 1 of left cable, work seed st over last 10 sts. Cont in pats as est for 6 rows more.
Next (dec) row (WS) Work 9 sts in seed st, p2tog tbl, p2, p2tog, work 19 sts as est, p2tog tbl, p2, p2tog, work 23 sts as est, p2tog tbl, p2, p2tog, work 25 sts as est, p2tog tbl, p2, p2tog, work 23 sts as est, p2tog tbl, p2, p2tog, work 19 sts as est, p2tog tbl, p2, p2tog, work 9 sts in seed st—151 sts. Work 5 rows as est.
Next (dec) row (WS) Work 8 sts in seed st, p2tog tbl, p2, p2tog, work 17 sts as est, p2tog tbl, p2, p2tog, work 21 sts as est, p2tog tbl, p2, p2tog, work 23 sts as

est, p2tog tbl, p2, p2tog, work 21, p2tog tbl, p2, p2tog, work 17 sts as est, p2tog tbl, p2, p2tog, work 8 sts in seed st—39 sts. Work 5 rows as est.
Next (dec) row (WS) Work 7 sts in seed st, p2tog tbl, p2, p2tog, work 15 sts as est, p2tog tbl, p2, p2tog, work 19 sts as est, p2tog tbl, p2, p2tog, work 21 sts as est, p2tog tbl, p2, p2tog, work 19 sts as est, p2tog tbl, p2, p2tog, work 15 sts as est, p2tog tbl, p2, p2tog, work 7 sts in seed st—127 sts. Work 5 rows as est.
Next (dec) row (WS) Work 6 sts in seed st, p2tog tbl, p2, p2tog, work 13 sts as est, p2tog tbl, p2, p2tog, work 17 sts as est, p2tog tbl, p2, p2tog, work 19 sts as est, p2tog tbl, p2, p2tog, work 17 sts as est, p2tog tbl, p2, p2tog, work 13 sts as est, p2tog tbl, p2, p2tog, work 6 sts in seed st—115 sts. Work 3 rows as est.
Next (dec) row (WS) Work 5 sts in seed st, p2tog tbl, p2, p2tog, work 11 sts as est, p2tog tbl, p2, p2tog, work 15 sts as est, p2tog tbl, p2, p2tog, work 17 sts as est, p2tog tbl, p2, p2tog, work 15 sts as est, p2tog tbl, p2, p2tog, work 11 sts as est, p2tog tbl, p2, p2tog, work 5 sts in

seed st—103 sts. Work 3 rows as est. Bind off.

BOBBLE BAND
With straight needles, cast on 9 sts. Beg with row 4 of bobble pat and work through row 8.
Rep rows 1–8 of bobble pat 15 times, then work rows 1–6 once. Bind off.

UPPER CABLED EDGE BAND
With straight needles, cast on 6 sts.
Set-up row (WS) K1, p4, k1.
Row 1 (RS) P1, 4-st LC, p1.
Row 2 K1, p4, k1.
Row 3 P1, k4, p1.
Row 4 K1, p4, k1.
Rep rows 1–4 58 times more.
Bind off.

FINISHING
Pin upper cabled edge band around cast-on edge of crown, matching at ends and center. Sew all around, taking care not to catch cable sts in seam. Sew center back seam of crown and upper cabled edge band. Pin upper edge of crown to beret top, matching center back seam to center of cast-on edge of top. Sew all around. Pin bobble band (p1, k1 edge) to lower edge of crown, matching center bobble to center of front panel. Sew all around. Weave in ends.

CELTIC MOTIF DETAILS
Leaving a long tail, work 3-st I-cord for approx 13"/33cm. Place sts on holder. Using photograph as a guide, starting at bottom of garter st diamond at center of hat (chart 1), pin I-cord to form Celtic shape around diamond. Lengthen or shorten the I-cord as needed. Use yarn ends from I-cord to tack down Celtic motif. Make motifs slightly smaller for front side panels (chart 2) by forming motif slightly inside garter st diamond. ⚘

St. Patrick's Day Necktie

Give him the luck of the Irish with this fanciful clover necktie—or leave out the clover and work the graduated stripe pattern in colors for any occasion.

◆

Designed by Amy Micallef

KNITTED MEASUREMENTS
Length 51"/129.5cm
Width 1¼"/3cm at narrowest point and 2½"/6.5cm at widest point

MATERIALS
■ 1 3½oz/100g skein (each approx 220yd/201m) of Universal Yarn *Deluxe Worsted* (100% wool) each in #3692 Christmas green (MC) and #61633 greenery (CC)

■ One set (5) size 4 (3.5mm) double-pointed needles (dpns) OR SIZE TO OBTAIN GAUGE

■ Stitch marker

GAUGE
24 sts and 28 rnds = 4"/10cm over St st using size 4 (3.5mm) needles.
TAKE TIME TO CHECK GAUGE.

NOTES
1) To work intarsia in the round, twist the two colors on the stitch before the chart, work chart, twist the two colors, and continue working around until 1 stitch before the chart. Run the color used in the chart across the back of the last row knitted. Do this for each row of the chart. The twists lock the yarn in place.
2) When changing colors pick up new color from under dropped color to prevent holes.
3) When working in the round, always read charts from right to left.

TIE
Cast on 30 sts with MC.
Pm and join to knit in the rnd, being careful not to twist sts.
Rnds 1 and 2 Purl.
Rnds 3–13 Knit.
Rnd 14 With CC, knit.
Rnd 15 With MC, knit.
Rnds 16–26 Work chart.
Rnd 27 With MC, knit.
Rnds 28 and 29 With CC, knit.
Rnds 30–41 With MC, knit.
Rnds 42–44 With CC, knit.
Rnds 45–55 With MC, knit.
Rnds 56–59 With CC, knit.
Rnds 60–69 With MC, knit.
Rnds 70–74 With CC, knit.
Rnds 75–83 -With MC, knit.
Rnds 84–89 With CC, knit.
Rnds 90–97 With MC, knit.
Rnds 98–104 With CC, knit.
Rnds 105 and 106 With MC, knit.
Rnd 107 [Ssk, k11, k2tog] twice.
Rnds 108–111 Knit.
Rnds 112–113 With CC, knit.
Rnd 114 [Ssk, k9, k2tog] twice.
Rnds 115–119 Knit.
Rnd 120 With MC, [ssk, k7, k2tog] twice—18 sts.
Rnds 121–125 Knit.
Rnds 126–134 With CC, knit.
Rnds 135–139 With MC, knit.
Rnds 140–149 With CC, knit.
Rnds 150–153 With MC, knit.
Rnds 154–164 With CC, knit.
Rnds 165–167 With MC, knit.
Rnds 168–179 With CC, knit.
Rnds 180 and 181 With MC, knit.
Rnds 182–194 With CC, knit.
Rnd 195 With MC, knit.
Rnds 196–209 With CC, knit.
Rnd 210 With MC, knit.
Rnds 211–223 With CC, knit.
Rnds 224 and 225 With MC, knit.
Rnds 226–237 With CC, knit.
Rnds 238–240 With MC, knit.
Rnds 241–251 With CC, knit.
Rnds 252–255 With MC, knit.
Rnds 256–265 With CC, knit.
Rnds 266–270 With MC, knit.

Rnds 271–279 With CC, knit.
Rnds 280–285 With MC, knit.
Rnds 286–293 With CC, knit.
Rnds 294–300 With MC, knit.
Rnds 301–307 With CC, knit.
Rnds 308–315 With MC, knit.
Rnds 316–321 With CC, knit.
Rnds 322–330 With MC, knit.
Rnds 331–335 With CC, knit.
Rnds 336–345 With MC, knit.
Rnds 346–349 With CC, knit.
Rnds 360–366 With MC, knit.
Rnds 367–369 Purl.

Divide sts onto two needles and bind off all sts using 3-needle bind-off.

FINISHING

Sew together cast-on end, and weave in all ends. Block gently. 🎀

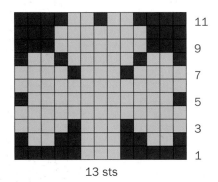

13 sts

COLOR AND STITCH KEY

■ Knit in MC

□ Knit in CC

Emerald Isle Lap Blanket

Snuggle up after a day of revelry in this cozy cabled blanket, knit in a shade of green that evokes the spirit of Ireland.

Designed by Kathy North

KNITTED MEASUREMENTS
Width approx 28"/71cm
Length approx 35"/89cm (after blocking)

MATERIALS
■ 4 3½oz/100g skeins (each approx 220yd/201m) Universal Yarn *Deluxe Worsted* (100% wool) in #12507 shamrock heather

■ Size 10 (6mm) circular needle, 32"/80cm long, OR SIZE TO OBTAIN GAUGE

■ Cable needle

■ Stitch markers

GAUGES
16 sts and 20 rows = 4"/10cm over St stitch on size 10 (6mm) needle.
15 sts and 25 rows = 4"/10cm over seed stitch on size 10 (6mm) needle.
21 sts and 20 rows = 4"/10cm over chart 3 cable pat on size 10 (6mm) needle.
TAKE TIME TO CHECK GAUGES.

NOTES
1) Afghan is worked flat in one piece on circular needle long enough to accommodate large number of stitches.
2) Place stitch markers between each panel pattern section as directed.
3) Charts are worked back and forth: read odd-numbered rows right to left, even-numbered (wrong-side) rows left to right.

STITCH GLOSSARY
4-st RC Sl next 2 sts to cn and hold to *back*, k2, k2 from cn.
4-st LC Sl next 2 sts to cn and hold to *front*, k2, k2 sts from cn.
4-st RPC Sl 2 sts to cn and hold to *back*, k2, p2 from cn.
4-st LPC Sl 2 sts to cn and hold to *front*, p2, k2 from cn.

SEED STITCH
(even number of sts)
Row 1 *K1, p1, rep from * across.
Row 2 *P1, k1, rep from * across.
Rep rows 1–2 for seed stitch.

AFGHAN
Cast on 112 sts loosely.
Rows 1–7 Work in seed st.
Row 8 (WS) [Work 8 sts seed st, pm] twice, work 6 sts seed st, pm, [work 8 sts seed st, pm] twice, work 36 sts seed st, pm, [work 8 sts seed st, pm] twice,

CHART 3

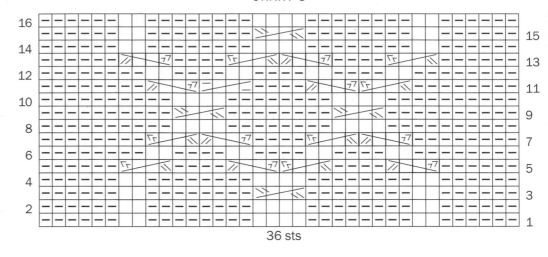

CHART 1

CHART 2

8 sts

8 sts

36 sts

STITCH KEY

☐ K on RS, p on WS

− P on RS, k on WS

4-st RC

4-st LC

4-st RPC

4-st LPC

work 6 sts seed st, pm, [work 8 sts seed st, pm] twice, omitting marker at end.

BEG CHARTS
Next row (RS) Work 8 sts seed st, work row 1 of chart 1, work 6 sts seed st, work row 1 of chart 2, work 8 sts seed st, work row 1 of chart 3, work 8 sts seed st, work row 1 of chart 1, work 6 sts seed st, work row 1 of chart 2, work 8 sts seed st.
NEXT ROW (WS) Work 8 sts seed st, work row 2 of chart 2, work 6 sts seed st, work row 2 of chart 1, work 8 sts seed st, work row 2 of chart 3, work 8 sts seed st, work row 2 of chart 2, work 6 sts seed st, work row 2 of chart 1, work 8 sts seed st. Work as est, alternating chart pats with seed st, until chart 3 has been worked a total of 11 times, ending with row 16. Work in seed st for 8 rows.

FINISHING
Bind off knitwise. Weave in all ends and block gently to measurements. 🎀

Easter Egg Toppers

Dyeing eggs can be fun, but once you've knit up these adorable cable caps, you'll want to dress your Easter eggs in them every year.

Designed by Jacqueline van Dillen

KNITTED MEASUREMENTS
Height approx 3½"/9cm without pompom

MATERIALS
■ 1 3 ½oz/100g skeins (each approx 220yd/201m) of Universal Yarn *Deluxe Worsted* (100% wool) each in #3608 marigold, #12177 hot fuschia, #41795 nectarine, and #3620 coral

■ One set (4) size 7 (4.5mm) double-pointed needles (dpns) OR SIZE TO OBTAIN GAUGE

■ Cable needle (cn)

■ Stitch marker

■ 1½"/4cm pompom maker

GAUGE
28 sts and 32 rows = 4"/10cm over cable pat using size 7 (4.5mm) needles. *TAKE TIME TO CHECK GAUGE.*

STITCH GLOSSARY
2-st RT Sl 2 sts to cn, hold to back, k2, k2 from cn.

CABLE PATTERN
(multiple of 4 sts)
Rnds 1–3 *P2, k2; rep from * around.
Rnd 4 *P2, 2-st RT; rep from* around.
Rep rnds 1–4 for cable pat.

EGG WARMER
(MAKE ONE IN EACH COLOR)
Cast on 32 sts and divide evenly over 3 dpns. Join and pm for beg of rnd.
Knit in cable pat for 2¾"/7cm.
Next rnd *P2tog, k2; rep from * around—24sts.
Work straight in pat for 3 rnds (k the knit sts and p the purl sts).
Next rnd K2tog around—12sts.
Knit 1 rnd and cut yarn, leaving a long tail. Thread yarn through rem sts and pull tightly.

POMPOM
(MAKE ONE IN EACH COLOR)
Wrap yarn densely around a 1½"/4cm pompom maker. Finish pompom, following package instructions.

FINISHING
Sew pompom to top of egg warmer.
Weave in ends.
Block gently to measurements. 🎀

Sunday in Spring Tea Cozy

Your teapot will look as festive as an Easter egg in this charming cozy, knit in a trellis pattern with delicate picot edges and a rosette on top.

Designed by Andrea Babb

KNITTED MEASUREMENTS
Circumference at widest point
20"/ 51cm
Depth 7"/18cm

MATERIALS
■ 1 3½oz/100g skein (each approx 220yd/201m) of Universal Yarn *Deluxe Worsted* (100% wool) each in #12270 natural (A) and #12277 periwinkle (B)

■ Size 4 (3.5mm) needles
OR SIZE TO OBTAIN GAUGE

■ One set (4) size 4 (3.5mm) double-pointed needles (dpns)

■ One snap fastener or hook & eye (choose one)

■ Stitch marker

GAUGE
26 sts and 32 rows to 4"/10cm in trellis chart pattern using size 4 (3.5mm) needles.
TAKE TIME TO CHECK GAUGE.

5-ST NUPP ST
Row 1 (RS) (K1, yo, k1, yo, k1) all in 1 st. Complete row.
Row 2 (WS) Purl 5 sts tog.

TEA COZY
UPPER RIGHT SECTION
Note Upper sections are worked from middle to top.
Picot edge With straight needles and B, cast on 69 sts. Work 3 rows in St st, beg and end with WS row.
Picot row (RS) *K1, k2tog, yo; rep from * to last 3 sts, k1, k2tog. Work 3 more rows in St st, ending with WS row.

BEG TRELLIS CHART
Row 1 (RS) K1, M1 (these are the first 2 sts of chart), join A, then begin working from RS row 1, st 3, of trellis chart, work to last st, M1, k1 (these are the last 2 sts of chart)—71 sts. Work remainder of trellis chart, dec and inc where indicated. Bind off on row 23, using B.

UPPER LEFT SECTION
Work picot edge same as for upper right section. Beg row 1 of trellis chart as above, but read chart from left to right on RS and right to left on WS. Work remainder of chart. Bind off on row 23, using B.

LOWER RIGHT SECTION
Note Bottom sections are worked from middle down.
With straight needles and B, cast on 71 sts.

Purl 1 row. Join A and beg trellis chart from right side. Work remainder of chart. Bind off on row 23, using B.

LOWER LEFT SECTION
With straight needles and B, cast on 71 sts. Purl 1 row. Join A and beg row 1 of trellis chart, but read chart from left to right on RS and right to left on WS. Work remainder of chart. Bind off on row 23, using B.

FINISHING
Wash and block four body pieces. Pin handle side of bottom sections together (arrange pieces so that the slight extension for the spout side is at the bottom of each piece). Sew 1"/2.5cm of side seam up from bottom on the handle side.

BOTTOM PICOT EDGE
With RS facing, straight needles and B, pick up 99 sts from left and right lower sections' bottom edge (do not pick up first and last bound-off sts). Work 3 rows in St st, ending with WS row. *K1, k2tog, yo; rep from * to last 3 sts, k1, k2tog. Work 3 more rows in St st. Bind off. Fold over and sew down picot edge all around, catching bound-off sts.
Pin handle side of upper sections together (arrange pieces so that the slight extension for the spout side is at the top of each piece). Sew 1"/2.5cm of handle side seam from top down.

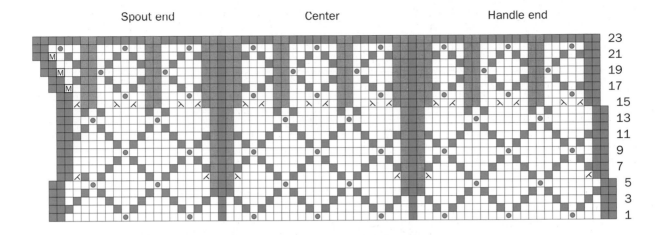

23
21
19
17
15
13
11
9
7
5
3
1

COLOR AND STITCH KEY

☐ K on RS, p on WS with A

■ K on RS, p on WS with B

☒ K2tog on RS, p2tog on WS

☒ Ssk on RS, p2tog tbl on WS

◉ 5-st nupp

Ⓜ M1

■ No stitch

UPPER PICOT EDGE

With RS facing, straight needles and B, pick up 101 sts from top edge of left and right upper sections. Work 3 rows in St st, ending with WS row. *K1, k2tog, yo; rep from * to last 2 sts, k2. Work 3 more rows in St st. Bind off. Fold over and sew down picot edge all around, catching bound-off sts.

HANDLE AND SPOUT OPENINGS

Fold under each side edge to the inside by 1 st and sew around each opening. Sew in any remaining yarn ends. Attach a snap or hook & eye closing to spout opening at bottom edge so that it overlaps slightly to hide closure.

TOP OF COZY

With RS facing, A and dpns, pick up and k 99 sts along inside of upper picot edge. Place marker and join for knitting in the round.
Rnd 1 *K7, k2tog; rep from * to end.
Rnd 2 and all even numbered rnds Knit.
Rnd 3 *K6, k2tog; rep from * to end.
Rnd 5 *K5, k2tog; rep from * to end.
Rnd 7 *K4, k2tog; rep from * to end.
Rnd 9 * K3, k2tog; rep from * to end.
Rnd 11 *K2, k2tog; rep from * to end.
Rnd 13 *K1, k2tog; rep from * to end.
Rnd 15 K2tog 9 times—9 sts. Trim yarn end to 8"/20.5cm and pull through 9 sts.

ROSETTE

Using straight needles and B, cast on 3 sts for larger petal.

Row 1 K1, yo, k2.
Row 2 and all RS rows Knit.
Row 3 K1, yo, k3.
Row 5 K1, yo, k4.
Row 7 K1, yo, k5.
Row 9 K1, yo, k6.
Row 11 K1, yo, k7.
Row 12 Bind off 6 sts. Knit rem sts.
Cut yarn, pull through 3 sts and fasten off.
Rep to make 4 larger petals total.
Using straight needles and B, cast on 2 sts for inner petal.
Row 1 K1, yo, k1.
Row 2 and all RS rows Knit.
Row 3 K1, yo, k2.
Row 5 K1, yo, k3.
Row 7 K1, yo, k4.
Row 9 K1, yo, k5.
Row 10 Bind off 5 sts, k rem sts.
Cut yarn, pull through 2 sts and fasten off.
Rep to make 4 inner petals total.
Gather lower edge of larger petals and sew to center of cozy top. Gather lower edge of inner petals and sew inside of larger petals to form rosette. 🎀

Chocolate Bunny Hat

Chocolate brown is the perfect color for this adorable Easter bunny, brightened up by pastel features and an orange carrot to munch on.

Designed by Kathy Perry

KNITTED MEASUREMENTS
Brim circumference (child's size)
21"/53.5cm

MATERIALS
■ 1 3½oz/100g skein (each 220yd/201m) of Universal Yarn *Deluxe Worsted* (100% wool) each in #12299 chocolate (MC), #12270 natural (A), #12298 butter (B), #12291 petit pink (C), and #71662 turquoise (D)

■ One pair size 9 (5.5mm) needles OR SIZE TO OBTAIN GAUGE

■ Stitch holder

■ Crochet hook (any size, for adding fringe)

■ Tapestry needle

■ Scrap yarn

GAUGE
17 sts and 24 rows = 4"/10cm over St st using size 9 (5mm) needles.
TAKE TIME TO CHECK GAUGE.

HAT
With MC, cast on 90 sts, leaving long end for sewing back seam. Work in St st until piece measures 3½"/9cm. Mark each side with scrap yarn for hem. Cont in St st until piece measures 13"/33cm from beg, end with WS row.

MAKE EARS
*K3, k2tog; rep from * 7 times more, k5—37 sts. Place rem 45 sts on st holder. Cont in St st until ear measures 7"/18cm. Cut yarn, leaving a 6"/15cm tail. Using tapestry needle, run yarn tail through live sts and remove from needle. Do not gather up. Transfer remaining sts from holder to needle, attach yarn and work second ear as first.

MAKE CARROT
Using one strand each of B and C held together, cast on 13 sts. Work in St st for 8 rows. Bind off.
Use purl side as RS and let sides curl naturally to shape into a tube. Cut four 6"/15cm pieces of D. Use tapestry needle to thread pieces through one end. Tie into knot and trim to desired length.

FINISHING
Sew back seam of hat, stopping at ears. Weave in ends.

EARS
Seam each ear into a tube and gather top sts tightly. Secure and sew in end.

HEM
Turn hem to inside at markers and sew in place. Turn up again to front for 2"/5cm roll and tack at back seam to hold in place.

TAIL
Make a 2"/5cm-diameter pompom using A, B, C, and D, and sew in place at back, just above hem.

FRINGE HAIR
Using two 24"/61cm pieces of D threaded into tapestry needle, make running sts over and under every couple of sts at beg of ears, starting and ending in front. Gather and tie so you have enough room to add fringe around stitches. Using A, B, C, and D, cut 16 pieces measuring 6"/15cm long. With crochet hook, add fringe into front gathering sts. Trim to desired length.

WHISKERS AND NOSE
Cut five 6"/15cm pieces of A. Tie all together with knot in center. Place at center front just above hem. Using C and tapestry needle, work satin st over knot to secure to hat. Trim whiskers to desired length.

EYES
Center and place 4–5 rows above nose with three sts in between. Using D and tapestry needle, work satin sts over 2 sts for each eye.

CARROT
Place completed piece into hem and tack in place (see photo). 🎀

Passover Yarmulkes

Three different designs—Fair Isle, seed stitch, and embroidered with Passover motifs—mean you'll find a yarmulke to suit any occasion and any man's (or woman's!) style.

Designed by Lori Steinberg

Embroidered Yarmulke

KNITTED MEASUREMENTS
Diameter 7"/18cm

MATERIALS
- 1 3½oz/100g skein (each approx 220yd/200m) of Universal Yarn *Deluxe Worsted* (wool) in #12174 ginseng (A)

- Small amounts in #12277 periwinkle (B), #91477 red oak (C), and #61633 greenery (D)

- One set (4) each sizes 5 and 6 (3.75 and 4mm) double-pointed needles (dpns) OR SIZE TO OBTAIN GAUGE

- Stitch markers

- Tapestry needle

GAUGE
20 sts and 32 rnds = 4" in St st using larger needles.
TAKE TIME TO CHECK GAUGE.

EMBROIDERED YARMULKE
With smaller needles and A, cast on 96 sts.
Place marker for beg of rnd and join, taking care not to twist sts.
Knit 3 rnds. Purl 1 rnd for turning ridge.
Change to larger needles.
Next rnd [K12, pm] 8 times around.
Work 4 rnds in St st.
Next (dec) rnd [SKP, k to 2 sts before marker, k2tog, sl marker] 8 times around.
Cont in St st and rep dec rnd every 4th rnd 4 times more—16 sts. Work 3 rnds even, k2tog around. Cut yarn and draw through rem sts twice.

FINISHING
Turn lower edge to WS along turning ridge and sew down.
With tapestry needle and B, working just above hem, work 6 French knots for grape cluster, between every other set of dec's, using photo as guide. With 2 strands of D held tog, work one straight st for grape stem above each grape cluster. With 4 strands of C held tog, work 1 French knot for pomegranate between the dec's not used for grapes. With 2 strands of C held tog, embroider 3 straight sts above pomegranate for pomegranate stalk. 🌿

Fair Isle Yarmulke

KNITTED MEASUREMENTS
Diameter 8"/20.5cm

MATERIALS
■ 1 3½oz/100g skein (each approx 220yd/200m) of Universal Yarn *Deluxe Worsted* (100% wool) each in #31953 neutral gray (MC) and #41795 nectarine (CC)

■ One set (4) each sizes 5 and 6 (3.75 and 4mm) double-pointed needles (dpns) OR SIZE TO OBTAIN GAUGE

■ Stitch marker

GAUGE
24 sts and 24 rnds = 4"/10cm over St st using larger needles.
TAKE TIME TO CHECK GAUGE.

FAIR ISLE YARMULKE
With smaller dpns and MC, cast on 114 sts. Place marker for beg of rnd and join, taking care not to twist sts.
Knit 4 rnds. Purl 1 rnd for turning ridge.
Next rnd [K18, p1] 6 times around.

BEG CHART
Rnd 1 Work stitch rep 6 times around.
Cont to work chart in this way until rnd 23 is complete.
Cut yarn, leaving a long tail. Draw tail through rem sts twice.

FINISHING
Turn lower edge to WS along turning ridge and sew down with MC.

COLOR AND STITCH KEY

☐	Knit in MC	▨	No stitch
⊟	Purl in MC	◿	P3tog
▧	Knit in CC		

Seed Stitch Yarmulke

KNITTED MEASUREMENTS
Diameter 9"/23cm

MATERIALS
■ 1 3½oz/100g skein (each approx 220yd/200m) of Universal Yarn *Deluxe Worsted* (wool) each in #12192 nitrox blue (A), #12507 shamrock heather (B), and #61633 greenery (C)

■ One set (4) each sizes 5 and 6 (3.75 and 4mm) double-pointed needles (dpns) OR SIZE TO OBTAIN GAUGE

■ Stitch marker

GAUGE
26 sts and 40 rnds = 4"/10cm over pat st using larger needles.
TAKE TIME TO CHECK GAUGE.

SEED STITCH
(over an odd number of sts)
Rnd 1 *K1, p1; rep from * to last st, k1.
Rnds 2–4 Purl the knit sts and knit the purl sts.
Rnd 5 Knit.
Rep rnds 1–5 for seed st.

SEED STITCH YARMULKE
With smaller needles and A, cast on 96 sts. Place marker for beg of rnd and join, taking care not to twist sts.
Knit 3 rnds. Purl 1 rnd for turning ridge.
Change to larger needles and B.
Next (inc) rnd Knit, inc 11 sts evenly around—107 sts.

BEG PAT ST
With B, work 5 rnds in pat st.
With C, work 4 rnds in pat st.
Next (dec) rnd Cont in pat st, dec 16 sts evenly around—97 sts.
Change to A.
Cont in pat st and rep dec rnd every 5th rnd 4 times—27 sts.
Change to smaller needles.
Work rnds 1 and 2 of pat st.
Next (dec) rnd [K1, k2tog] 9 times—18 sts.
Rep rnds 1 and 2 of part st.
Next dec rnd [K2tog] 9 times.
Cut yarn and thread through rem sts twice.

FINISHING
Fold lower edge to WS along turning ridge and sew down.

FAIR ISLE YARMULKE

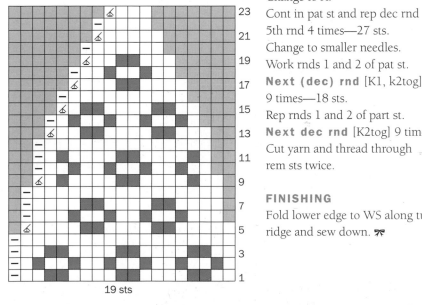

19 sts

for Mom,
made with
Love

Mother's Day Ruffled Scarf

A scarf that combines seed stitch ruffles with sparingly placed eyelets is the perfect blend of warmth and femininity. Short rows are used to create the ruffles.

Designed by Jacqueline Jewett

KNITTED MEASUREMENTS
Width approx 11"/28cm
Length approx 60"/152.5cm

MATERIALS
■ 3 3½oz/100g skeins (each approx 220yd/201m) of Universal Yarn *Deluxe Worsted* (100% wool) in #12234 flintstone

❀ One pair size 7 (4.5mm) needles OR SIZE TO OBTAIN GAUGE

GAUGE
20 sts and 24 rows = 4"/10cm in St st and seed st using size 7 needles.
TAKE TIME TO CHECK GAUGE.

STITCH GLOSSARY
RT (right twist) Skip next st on LH needle, knit 2nd st in front of the skipped st, then knit skipped st, sl both sts from needle.
LT (left twist) With RH needle behind LH needle, skip next st on LH needle, knit 2nd st tbl, then knit skipped st in front loop, sl both sts from needle.

SEED STITCH
(odd number of sts)
Row 1 (RS) K1, *p1, k1; rep from * to end.
Row 2 (WS) Purl the knit sts and knit the purl sts as they appear.
Repeat row 2 for seed st.

SCARF
Cast on 1 st.
Row 1 (RS) K1.
Row 2 (WS) K1.
Row 3 [P1, k1, p1] into 1 stitch—3 sts.
Row 4 P1, k1, p1.
Row 5 [K1, p1] into 1st st, k1, [p1, k1] into last st—5 sts.
Row 6 K1, p1, k1, p1, k1.
Row 7 [P1, k1] into first st, cont in seed st to last st, [k1, p1] into last st—7 sts.
Row 8 *P1, k1; rep from * to last st, p1.
Rows 9–25 Cont in seed st and inc 1 st each end of RS rows as est until there are 25 sts.
Row 26 (foundation row for center panel) Work seed st over first 11 sts, p3, work seed st over rem 11 sts.
Row 27 Inc 1 st as est, work in seed st to center 5 sts, k5, work in seed st to last st and inc 1 as est—27 sts.
Row 28 Work seed st over first 11 sts, p5, work seed st over rem 11 sts.
Row 29 Work first 11 sts in seed st, RT, yo, k1, yo, LT, work seed st over last 11 sts—29 sts.
Row 30 and all WS rows Work seed st over first and last 11 sts, and on center panel purl all sts.

BEG SHORT-ROW RUFFLE
Row 31 Work seed st over first 11, turn, slip the first st knitwise, work in seed st to end, turn, work in seed st over 11 sts, RT, yo, k3, yo, LT, work 11 sts in seed st. Turn. Work in seed st over 11 sts, turn, slip the first st knitwise, work in seed st to end—31 sts. Work WS row.
Row 33 Work seed st and ruffle over first 11 sts, RT, yo, k5, yo, LT, work seed st and ruffle over last 11 sts—33 sts.
Row 35 Work seed st and ruffle over first 11 sts, RT, yo, k7, yo, LT, work seed st and ruffle over last 11 sts—35 sts.
Note Cont ruffled edge pattern as est every RS row. The following instructions will be for center panel *only*, until decreasing for end of scarf.
Row 37 (center panel) RT, yo, k3, yo, SK2P, yo, k3, yo, LT—15 sts center panel, 37 sts total.
Row 39 RT, yo, k2, k2tog, yo, k3, yo, ssk, k2, yo, LT.

Row 41 RT, yo, k5, yo, SK2P, yo, k5, yo, LT.

Rows 43, 45, and 47 RT, yo, work in St st to last 2 sts of center panel, yo, LT—25 sts center panel, 47 sts total.

Row 49 RT, yo, k3, yo, SK2P, yo, k9, yo, SK2P, yo, k3, yo, LT.

Row 51 RT, yo, k2, k2tog, yo, k3, yo, ssk, k5, k2tog, yo, k3, yo, ssk, k2, yo, LT.

Row 53 RT, yo, k5, yo, SK2P, yo, k9, yo, SK2P, yo, k5, yo, LT—31 sts center panel, 53 sts total.

Rows 55, 57, and 59 RT, work in St st to last 2 sts of center panel, LT.

Row 61 RT, k1, k2tog, yo, k9, yo, SK2P, yo, k9, yo, ssk, k1, LT.

Row 63 RT, k3, yo, ssk, k5, k2tog, yo, k3, yo, ssk, k5, k2tog, yo, k3, LT.

Row 65 Work as row 59.

Rows 67, 69, and 71 RT, work in St st to last 2 sts of center panel, LT.

Row 73 RT, k6, yo, SK2P, yo, k9, yo, SK2P, yo, k6, LT.

Row 75 RT, k4, k2tog, yo, k3, yo, ssk, k5, k2tog, yo, k3, yo, ssk, k4, LT.

Row 77 Work as for row 73.

Row 78 Work a WS row.

Rep rows 55–78 ten times more, then work rows 55–72 once.

END RUFFLE

Row 1 (RS) Work 11 sts in seed st, RT, ssk, k4, yo, SK2P, yo, k9, yo, SK2P, yo, k4, k2tog, LT, work seed st to end—51 sts.

Row 2 and all WS rows Work seed st over first and last 11 sts, and on center panel purl all sts.

Row 3 Work 11 sts in seed st, RT, ssk, k1, k2tog, yo, k3, yo, ssk, k5, k2tog, yo, k3, yo, ssk, k1, k2tog, LT, work seed st to end—49 sts.

Row 5 Work 11 sts in seed st, RT, ssk, k2, yo, SK2P, yo, k9, yo, SK2P, yo, k2, k2tog, LT, work seed st to end—47 sts.

Rows 7, 9, and 11 Work 11 sts in seed st, RT, ssk, knit to last 4 sts of center panel, k2tog, LT, work seed st to end—41 sts.

Row 13 Work 11 sts in seed st, RT, ssk, k4, yo, SK2P, yo, k4, k2tog, LT, work seed st to end—39 sts.

Row 15 Work 11 sts in seed st, RT, ssk, k1, k2tog, yo, k3, yo, ssk, k1, k2tog, LT, work seed st to end—37 sts.

Row 17 Work 11 sts in seed st, RT, ssk, k2, yo, SK2P, yo, k2, k2tog, LT, work seed st to end—35 sts.

Rows 19, 21, and 23 Work 11 sts in seed st, RT, ssk, knit to last 4 sts of center panel, k2tog, LT, work seed st to end—29 sts.

Row 25 Work 11 sts in seed st, RT, SK2P, LT, work seed st to end—27 sts.

Row 27 Work 11 sts in seed st, ssk, k1, k2tog, work seed st to end—25 sts.

Row 29 ssk, work in seed st to last 2 sts, k2tog—23 sts.

Next row (WS) Work in seed st to end. Rep last 2 rows until 3 sts rem, k3tog, bind off.

FINISHING

Weave in ends. Block gently to measurements. 🎀

Mom's Cozy Slipper Socks

What better way to pamper Mom—or yourself—than with a warm pair of slippers?
A ribbon threaded through eyelets complements the cozy cable pattern.

Designed by Jacqueline van Dillen

SIZE
Women's shoe size 7/8

KNITTED MEASUREMENTS
Length 9"/23cm
Height 4½"/11.5cm

MATERIALS
■ 1 3½oz/100g skein (each approx 220yd/201m) of Universal Yarn *Deluxe Worsted* (100% wool) in #12189 baby blue

■ One pair size 7 (4.5mm) needles OR SIZE TO OBTAIN GAUGE

■ 2¼yd/2m of ½" satin ribbon

■ Stitch markers

GAUGE
24 sts and 28 rows = 4"/10cm over cable pattern using size 7 (4.5mm) needles.
TAKE TIME TO CHECK GAUGE.

CABLE PATTERN
Row 1 (RS) K1, *p2, k3; rep from * to last 3 sts, p2, k1.
Rows 2 and 4 P1, *k2, p3; rep from * to last 3 sts, k2, p1.
Row 3 K1, *p2, sl 1 wyib, k2, yo, psso the k2 and yo; rep from * to last 3 sts, p2, k1.
Rep rows 1–4 for cable pat.

SLIPPER (MAKE 2)
Cast on 89 sts and mark the center st.
Rows 1–11 Work in cable pat. On each WS (even) row, inc 1 st in the first st, the st before the marker, the st after the marker, and the last st (keep sts in pattern, 4 sts inc per row)—109 sts.
Rows 12–14 Continue in pat, remove marker.
Row 15 Continue in pat, placing markers after 51 sts and 58 sts.
Row 16 Work to 3 sts before 1st marker, k3tog, sm, work to 2nd marker, sm, k3tog, work to end.
Repeat row 16 every other row 6 times more—81 sts.
Row 29 Continue in pat, removing markers.
Row 30 Work first 39 sts, pm, p3, pm, work 39 sts.

Row 31 (eyelet row) K1, *p2, k2tog, yo, k1; rep from * to 3 sts before marker, p1, p2tog, yo, k3, yo, p2tog, p1, **k2tog, yo, k1, p2, rep from ** to last st, k1.
Row 32 Work all sts as they appear, purling the yos and removing markers. Bind off.

FINISHING
Weave in ends. Fold slipper in half and sew the sole and back together. Weave ribbon through eyelet row and tie in the front of each sock. ✄

Bouquet Shawl

This unique shawl knits up quickly with two strands of yarn, but its appliqué flowers, modern hues, and generous fringe make a big impact.

Designed by Joan McGowan-Michael

KNITTED MEASUREMENTS
Width approx 53"/134.5cm
Height approx 25"/63.5cm
(excluding fringe)

MATERIALS
■ 4 3½oz/100g skeins (each approx 220yd/201m) of Universal Yarn *Deluxe Worsted* (100% wool) in #12502 smoke heather (MC)

■ 1 3½oz/100g skein (approx 270yd/247m) of Universal Yarn *Renew Wool* (65% virgin wool/35% repurposed wool) each in #113 garnet, #109 stone, #110 flint, and #101 sand

■ Size 9 (5.5mm) circular needle, 40"/100cm long, OR SIZE TO OBTAIN GAUGE

■ One set size 7 (4.5mm) double-pointed needles (dpns)

■ Size G/6 (4mm) crochet hook (for fringe)

■ Stitch markers

■ Tapestry needle

GAUGE
13 sts and 22 rows = 4"/10 cm
over St st with size 9 (5.5mm) needles and yarn held doubled.
TAKE TIME TO CHECK GAUGE.

NOTES
1) Yarn is held double for body of shawl and single for appliqué pieces.
2) Each flower is knit in 2 colors (see photo).

SHAWL
With larger needles and 2 strands of MC held tog, cast on 5 sts.
Row 1 (RS) [K1, yo] twice, pm, k1, pm, [yo, k1] twice—9 sts.
Row 2 Purl.
Row 3 K1, yo, k to marker, yo, sl marker, k1, sl marker, yo, k to 1 st rem, yo, k1—13 sts.
Row 4 Purl.
Rows 5–12 Rep rows 3–4 four times more—29 sts.
Row 13 [K1, yo] twice, *k2tog, yo, rep from * until marker, sl marker, k1, sl marker, *yo, k2tog, rep from * until 2 sts rem, [yo, k1] twice.
Row 14 Purl.
Rep rows 3–14 seven times more—201 sts.
Rep rows 13–14 twice more—209 sts.
Bind off.

APPLIQUÉS
FLOWERS (MAKE 3)
Using dpns, cast on 5 sts. Join to work in the rnd, being careful not to twist, pm at beg of rnd.
Rnd 1 [K1, m1] 5 times—10 sts.
Rnd 2 and all even-numbered rnds Knit.
Rnd 3 [K1, m1] 10 times—20 sts.
Rnd 5 [K2, m1] 10 times—30 sts. Change color.
Rnd 7 With new color, [k3, m1] 10 times—40 sts.
Rnd 9 [K4, m1] 10 times—50 sts.
Row 11 K10, turn.
Row 12 and rem even-numbered rows Purl.
Row 13 Ssk, k6, k2tog.
Row 15 Ssk, k4, k2tog.
Row 17 Ssk, k2, k2tog.
Row 19 Ssk, k2tog.
Row 20 P2tog, fasten off and cut yarn. Reattach yarn for next petal. Work over 10 sts, starting with row 11. Repeat until you have worked all sts and have a total of 5 petals.

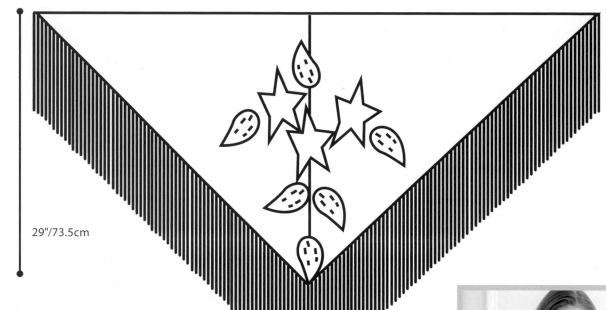

54"/147cm

29"/73.5cm

LEAVES (MAKE 7)

Using dpns, cast on 4 sts.

Row 1 Purl.

Row 2 (RS) K2, yo, k2.

Row 3 and all WS rows Purl.

Row 4 K2, yo, k1, yo, k2—7 sts.

Row 6 K3, yo, k1, yo, k3—9 sts.

Row 8 K4, yo, k1, yo, k4—11 sts.

Row 10 K5, yo, k1, yo, k5—13 sts.

Row 12 Knit.

Row 14 Ssk, k9, k2tog—11 sts.

Row 16 Ssk, k7, k2tog—9 sts.

Row 18 Ssk, k5, k2tog—7 sts.

Row 20 Ssk, k3, k2tog—5 sts.

Row 22 Ssk, k1, k2tog—3 sts

Row 24 Sl 1, k2tog, psso. Fasten off.

FINISHING

Steam press flowers and leaves. Arrange as shown in schematic and pin in place. Stitch to shawl, weaving in all ends.

FRINGE

Cut 100 pieces of each color of yarn, 16"/40.5cm long. Fold each strand in half and attach randomly to bottom edge of shawl by pulling loop of yarn through stitch, threading ends of fringe through the loop, and pulling tight.

Block entire shawl lightly. ✼

Lovely Lacy Clutch

Mom will love carrying this special occasion clutch throughout the year for evening get-togethers and nights on the town.

Designed by Grace Verderosa

KNITTED MEASUREMENTS
Width approx 12"/30.5cm
Height approx 5½"/14cm

MATERIALS
■ 1 3½oz/100g skein (each approx 220yd/201m) of Universal Yarn *Deluxe Worsted* (100% wool) in #71006 white ash

■ One pair size 7 (4.5mm) needles OR SIZE TO OBTAIN GAUGE

■ Snap closure

■ ½yd/.5m fabric for lining (optional)

■ Sewing needle and thread in matching color (optional)

GAUGE
18 sts and 28 rows = 4"/10cm over St st using size 7 (4.5mm) needles. TAKE TIME TO CHECK GAUGE.

LACE PATTERN
(multiple of 10 sts plus 7)
Row 1 (RS) K3, *p1, yo, k3, SK2P, k3, yo; rep from * to last 4 sts, p1, k3.
Rows 2, 4, and 6 K3, *k1, p9; rep from * to last 4 sts, k4.
Row 3 K3, *p1, k1, yo, k2, SK2P, k2, yo, k1; rep from * to last 4 sts, p1, k3.
Row 5 K3, *p1, k2, yo, k1, SK2P, k1, yo, k2; rep from * to last 4 sts, p1, k3.
Row 7 K3, *p1, k3, yo, SK2P, yo, k3; rep from * to last 4 sts, p1, k3.
Row 8 K3, *k1, p9; rep from * to last 4 sts, k4.
Rep rows 1–8 for lace pat.

CLUTCH
Cast on 57 sts.
Work 4 rows in garter st (k every row). Change to lace pat and work for 3 complete repeats. Knit 4 rows. Keeping 3 sts each side in garter st, change to St st and work for 5"/12.5cm. Knit 4 rows. Keeping 3 sts each side in garter st, change to St st and work for 4½"/11.5cm. Knit 4 rows. Bind off.

Finishing
Weave in ends. Fold and sew side seams. Line bag as foll (optional):

LINING
Cut fabric 12"/30.5cm square and fold back 1"/2.5cm on all sides. Sew side seams with right sides together and attach lining to bag at top opening with needle and thread.

POCKET
Cut fabric 9"/23cm x 5"/12.5cm. Fold back 1"/.5cm on all sides and fold in half, wrong sides together. Sew to lining in center front of lining. Sew snap to inside center of clutch. ✾

Sweet and Slouchy Hat

A bright shade of pink and a flower motif constructed from cables on the crown make this comfy hat the perfect springtime gift for Mom.

Designed by Kim Haesemeyer

KNITTED MEASUREMENTS
Brim circumference
(unstretched) 18"/45.5cm
Brim diameter 10"/25.5cm

MATERIALS
■ 1 3½oz/100g skein (each approx 220yd/201m) of Universal Yarn *Deluxe Worsted* (100% wool) in #12177 hot fuschia

■ One each sizes 5 (3.75mm) and 6 (4mm) circular needle, each 16"/41cm long, OR SIZE TO OBTAIN GAUGE

■ One set (4) size 6 (4mm) double-pointed needles (dpns)

■ Stitch marker

■ Cable needle (cn)

GAUGE
20 stitches and 26 rnds = 4"/10cm over St st using size 6 (4mm) circular needle.
TAKE TIME TO CHECK GAUGE.

STITCH GLOSSARY
double inc Knit into the front, back, then front of st (inc 2 sts).
M1P Make 1 purl st.
3-st RPC Sl 1 st to cn and hold in *back*, k2, p1 from cn.

3-st LPC Sl 2 sts to cn and hold in *front*, p1, k2 from cn.
4-st RC Sl 2 sts to cn and hold in *back*, k2, k2 from cn.
4-st LC Sl 2 sts to cn and hold in *front*, k2, k2 from cn.
4-st RPC Sl 1 st to cn and hold in *back*, k3, p1 from cn.
4-st LPC Sl 3 sts to cn and hold in *front*, p1, k3 from cn.
5-st RC Sl 3 sts to cn and hold in *back*, k2, [p1, k2] from cn.
5-st LC Sl 3 sts to cn and hold in *front*, k2, [p1, k2] from cn.
5-st RPC Sl 3 sts to cn and hold in *back*, k2, p3 from cn.
5-st LPC Sl 2 sts to cn and hold in *front*, p3, k2 from cn.

NOTE
When working in the round, always read charts from right to left.

HAT
With smaller needle, cast on 144 sts. Pm and join, being careful not to twist sts. Work rnds 1–7 of chart, repeating it 8 times around. Note the first row starts with 18 sts per repeat. Change to larger needles. Work rnds 8–58 of chart, switching to dpns when needed.

FINISHING
Cut yarn, leaving a long tail for weaving. Thread through remaining sts and pull tight. Weave in ends. Block lightly if desired. ✂

Father's Day Multicolor Scarf

A self-striping yarn combines with a slip stitch colorwork pattern to stunning effect, creating a fabric that's thick and warm.

Designed by Mari Tobita

KNITTED MEASUREMENTS
Width approx 6½"/16.5cm
Length approx 65½"/166cm

MATERIALS
■ 2 3½oz/100g skeins (each approx 220yd/201m) of Universal Yarn *Deluxe Worsted* (100% wool) in #12278 mallard (MC)

■ 2 3½oz/100g skeins (each approx 220yd/201m) of Universal Yarn *Deluxe Worsted Long Print* (100% wool) in #01 sea + sand (CC)

■ One pair size 9 (5.5mm) needles OR SIZE TO OBTAIN GAUGE

GAUGES
17.5 sts and 23 rows = 4"/10cm over St st using size 9 (5.5mm) needles.
19 sts and 33.5 rows = 4"/10cm over slip stitch pat using size 9 (5.5mm) needles.
TAKE TIME TO CHECK GAUGES.

NOTE
Slip 1 purlwise with yarn in back unless otherwise specified.

SLIP STITCH PATTERN
Row 1 (RS) With MC, K2, [sl 1, k1, sl 1, k5] 3 times, sl 1, k1, sl 1, k2.
Row 2 (WS) K2, [wyif sl 1, p1, wyif sl 1, k5] 3 times, wyif sl 1, p1, wyif sl 1, k2.
Row 3 With CC, k3, [sl 1, k7] 3 times, sl 1, k3.
Row 4 K2, [p1, wyif sl 1, p1, k5] 3 times, p1, sl1 wyif, p1, k2.
Row 5 Rep row 1.
Row 6 Rep row 2.
Row 7 Rep row 3.
Row 8 Rep row 4.
Row 9 With MC, k6, [sl 1, k1, sl 1, k5] 3 times, k1.
Row 10 K1, [k5, wyif sl 1, p1, wyif sl 1] 3 times, k6.
Row 11 With CC, [k7, sl 1] 3 times, k7.
Row 12 K6, [p1, wyif sl 1, p1, k5] 3 times, k1.
Row 13 Rep row 9.
Row 14 Rep row 10.
Row 15 Rep row 11.
Row 16 Rep row 12.

SCARF
With MC, cast on 31 sts. Knit 4 rows.
Work rows 3–16 of slip stitch pattern once, then rows 1–16 33 times.
With MC, knit 4 rows.
Bind off purlwise.

FINISHING
Weave in ends. Block piece to measurements. 🎀

Grandpa's Eyeglass Case

He can relax with a book and pull out his reading glasses in style with this case featuring houndstooth checks, a durable felted finish, and a button closure.

Designed by Barb Brown

FINISHED MEASUREMENTS

Approx 9" x 8"/23cm x 20.5cm, before felting
Approx 6½" x 3½"/16.5cm x 9cm, after felting

MATERIALS

■ 1 3½oz/100g skein (each approx 220yd/201m) of Universal Yarn *Deluxe Worsted* (100% wool) each in #12176 teal viper (A) and #12508 woodsy heather (B)

■ One set size 7 (4.5mm) double-pointed needles (dpns) OR SIZE TO OBTAIN GAUGE

■ One ½" button

■ Tapestry needle

GAUGE

20 sts and 20 rows = 4"/10 cm over St st using size 7 (4.5mm) needles. *TAKE TIME TO CHECK GAUGE.*

EYEGLASS CASE

With A, cast on 40 sts. Join in the rnd, being careful not to twist, pm for beg of rnd. Knit one rnd. Join B, work rnds 1–14 of chart twice, then work rnds 1–8 (work each row of chart five times for each rnd). Cont in A only. Knit one rnd, foll by one purl rnd. Bind off 20 sts and cont working 20 sts flat for rem.

FLAP

Row 1 Knit.
Row 2 Sl 1, p2tog, p to last 3 sts, p2tog, k1.
Row 3 Sl 1, k to end.
Rows 4–10 Rep rows 2 and 3 until 10 sts rem, ending with row 2.
Row 11 K4, bind off 2 sts, k4.
Row 12 P1, p2tog, p1, cast on 2, p to last 3 sts, p2tog, p1.
Row 13 Sl 1, k to end.
Row 14 Rep row 2.
Bind off rem 6 sts.

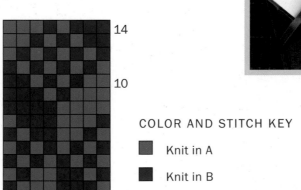

14
10
1

8-st rep

COLOR AND STITCH KEY

Knit in A
Knit in B

FINISHING

Sew bottom seam using mattress stitch.
Weave in all ends.
Felt piece to size. (Agitate with hot water and rinse with cold.) Pull into shape.
Be careful to keep buttonhole open.
Sew on button. ✄

Outdoorsman Socks

Whether he's fishing, working in the yard, or just settling in on the porch with a cup of coffee, these rugged striped socks will keep Dad's feet warm and comfy.

Designed by Cheryl Murray

SIZE
Men's shoe size 11

KNITTED MEASUREMENTS
Leg circumference 6½"/16.5cm
with rib relaxed
Foot circumference 9"/23cm
with rib relaxed
Leg length 8½"/21.5cm
Foot length 11"/28cm
Heel height 2½"/6.5cm

MATERIALS
■ 1 3½oz/100g skein (approx 270yd/247m) of Universal Yarn *Renew Wool* (65% virgin wool/35% repurposed wool) each in #104 shale (A) and #111 russet (B)

■ One set (5) size 6 (4mm) double-pointed needles (dpns) OR SIZE TO OBTAIN GAUGE

■ Cable needle (cn)

■ Stitch markers

GAUGE
24 sts and 32 rows = 4"/10cm over St st in the rnd using size 6 (4mm) needles.
TAKE TIME TO CHECK GAUGE.

STITCH GLOSSARY
3-st RC Sl 2 sts to cn, hold to *back*, k1, k2 from cn.
3-st LC Sl 1 st to cn, hold to *front*, k2, k1 from cn.

SOCK (MAKE 2)
With A, cast on 52 sts loosely. Divide sts evenly on 4 dpns. Join in the rnd, being careful not to twist, pm at beg of rnd.

CUFF
Rnd 1 K1, *p2, k2; repeat from *, end p2, k1. Cont in rib pat as established until cuff measures 2½"/6.5cm from beg.

LEG
Next rnd (set-up rnd) K1, [p2, k2] 5 times, p2, pm, k6, pm, [p2, k2] 5 times, p2, k1.
Rnd 1 With B, work in established pat to first marker, sl marker, work 6 sts of cable chart, sl marker, work to end in established pat.
Rnds 2–10 Cont working rib pat as established and working sts between markers according to cable chart, changing colors as indicated.
Rep rnds 1–10 five times more. Work rnds 1–2 once more.

LEFT HEEL FLAP
With WS facing and A, p26 on needles 3 and 4. Work back and forth over 26 sts as foll:
Row 1 (RS) *Sl 1 wyib, k1; rep from * to end.

Row 2 Sl 1 wyib, p to end.
Rep these 2 rows until 24 rows are complete. Heel flap should measure 2½"/6.5cm.

RIGHT HEEL FLAP
With RS facing and A, work 26 sts on needles 1 and 2 as foll:
Row 1 (RS) *Sl 1 wyib, k1; rep from * to end.
Row 2 Sl 1 wyib, p to end.
Rep these 2 rows until 24 rows are complete. Heel flap should measure 2½"/6.5cm.

TURN HEEL
Row 1 (RS) K14, ssk, k1. Turn.
Row 2 (WS) Sl 1, p3, p2tog, p1. Turn.
Row 3 Sl 1, k4, ssk, k1. Turn.
Row 4 Sl 1, p5, p2tog, p1. Turn.
Row 5 Sl 1, k6, ssk, k1. Turn.
Row 6 Sl 1, p7, p2tog, p1. Turn.
Row 7 Sl 1, k8, ssk, k1. Turn.
Row 8 Sl 1, p9, p2tog, p1. Turn.
Row 9 Sl 1, k10, ssk, k1. Turn.
Row 10 Sl 1, p11, p2tog, p1. Turn.
Row 11 Sl 1, k12, ssk. Turn.
Row 12 Sl 1, p12, p2tog. Turn—14 sts.

Dad's Golf Club Covers

Surprise him after a day on the links with these fun cozies. Each of the four color patterns fits a different size club and is topped with a pompom.

Designed by Lori Steinberg

KNITTED MEASUREMENTS
Diameter approx 7½"/19cm
Length (excluding pompoms) approx 12"/30.5cm

MATERIALS
■ 1 3½oz/100g skein (each approx 220yd/200m) of Universal Yarn *Deluxe Worsted* (100% wool) each in #12501 oatmeal heather (A), #12192 nitrox blue (B), #61633 greenery (C), and #3677 cobalt (D)

■ One set (4) size 8 (5mm) double-pointed needles (dpns) OR SIZE TO OBTAIN GAUGE

■ Stitch marker

GAUGE
22 sts and 22 rnds = 4"/10cm over chart 1 pat using size 8 (5mm) needles. *TAKE TIME TO CHECK GAUGE.*

K1, P2 RIB
(multiple of 3 sts)
Rnd 1 *K1, p2; rep from * around.
Rep rnd 1 for k1, p2 rib.

7 OR 9 WOOD COVER
With A, cast on 39 sts. Place marker for beg of rnd and join, taking care not to twist sts.
Work in k1, p2 rib until piece measures 4"/10cm from beg, inc 1 st at end of last rnd—40 sts.

BEG CHART 1
Rnd 1 Work 20 sts of chart 1 twice around.
Cont to work chart in this way until rnd 38 is complete. Cut B.
Next (dec) rnd With A, k1, *k3tog; rep from * around—14 sts.
Next (dec) rnd [K2tog] 7 times around.
Cut A, leaving a long tail. Thread tail through open sts to close.

FINISHING
Make a 2"/5cm pompom with A, B, and C and sew to top of cover. Weave in ends.

5 WOOD COVER
Work as for 7 or 9 wood cover to chart 1.
BEG CHARTS 1 AND 2
Note When working chart 1, use the colors for the rnd of chart 2 being worked, with A as the background color and the 2nd color for the motif.
Next row Work chart 2 over 20 sts, work chart 1 over 20 sts.
Cont to work chart in this way through rnd 32. Complete as for 7 or 9 wood cover.

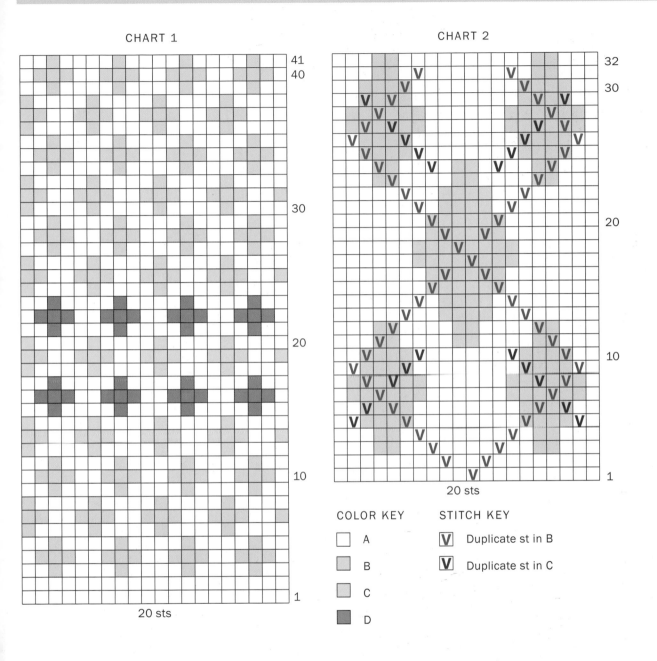

CHART 1

20 sts

CHART 2

20 sts

COLOR KEY

- A
- B
- C
- D

STITCH KEY

- [V] Duplicate st in B
- [V] Duplicate st in C

FINISHING

With C and D and yarn needle, work duplicate stitch foll chart.

With D, make a 2"/5cm pompom and sew to top of cover. Weave in ends.

3 WOOD COVER

Work as for 7 or 9 wood cover to chart 1.

BEG CHARTS 1 AND 3

Note When working chart 1, use the colors for the rnd of chart 3 being worked, with A as the background color and the 2nd color for the motif.

Next row Work chart 3 over 20 sts, work chart 1 over 20 sts.

Cont to work chart in this way through rnd 41. Complete as for 7 or 9 wood cover.

FINISHING

With C and yarn needle, work duplicate stitch foll chart.

With C, make a 2"/5cm pompom and sew to top of cover. Weave in ends.

CHART 3

CHART 4

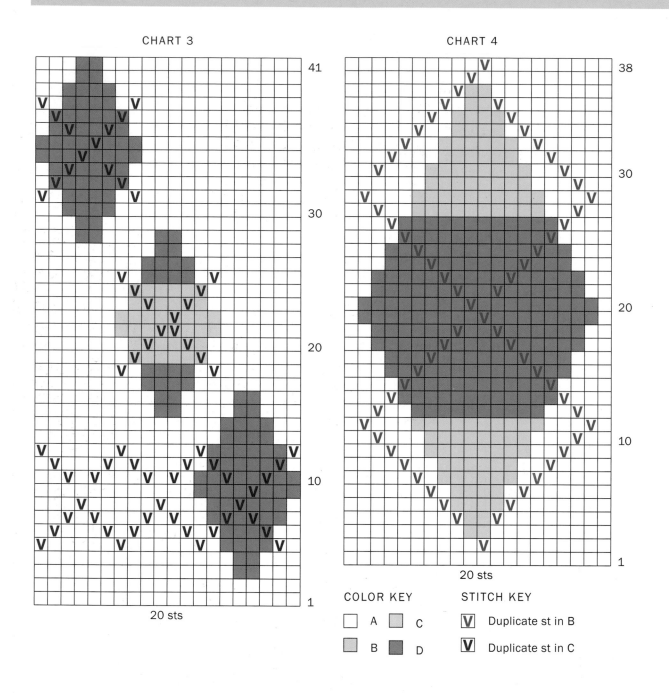

20 sts

20 sts

COLOR KEY

☐ A   ▨ C

▨ B   ▨ D

STITCH KEY

Ⅴ Duplicate st in B

Ⅴ Duplicate st in C

DRIVER COVER
Work as for 7 or 9 wood cover to chart 1.

BEG CHARTS 1 AND 5
Note When working chart 1, use the colors for the rnd of chart 5 being worked,

with A as the background color and the 2nd color for the motif.
Next row Work chart 5 over 20 sts, work chart 1 over 20 sts.
Cont to work chart in this way through rnd 38. Complete as for 7 or 9 wood cover.

FINISHING
With B and yarn needle, work duplicate stitch foll chart.
With B, make a 2"/5cm pompom and sew to top of cover. Weave in ends. ✄

Party Time Cupcakes

Indulge your sweet tooth in a healthy way with these sweetly colored cupcakes.
Use them to decorate a child's birthday party!

◆

Designed by Lori Steinberg

KNITTED MEASUREMENTS
Height approx 4"/10cm
(after stufffing)
Top circumference 10"/25.5cm
(after stuffing)
Base circumference 6"/15cm
(after stuffing)

MATERIALS
■ 1 3 ½oz/100g skein or small amount
(each approx 220yd/201m) of Universal
Yarn *Deluxe Worsted* (100% wool)
each in #12298 butter (A), #12257
pulp (B), #12291 petit pink (C), and
#12179 dark oak (D)

■ One set (4) each sizes 4 and 7 (3.5
and 4.5mm) double-pointed needles
(dpns) OR SIZE TO OBTAIN GAUGE

■ Stitch marker

■ Button embellishments, sewing
needle and thread

■ Polyester stuffing

■ Cardboard

GAUGE
22 sts and 24 rnds = 4"/10cm over St st
using larger needles.
TAKE TIME TO CHECK GAUGE.

CUPCAKE
With smaller dpns and A, cast on 28 sts.
Place marker for beg of rnd and join,
taking care not to twist sts.
Next rnd *K1, p1; rep from * around for
k1, p1 rib.
Rep last rnd twice more.
Next (inc) rnd *K1, p1, M1 p-st; rep
from * around—42 sts.
Next rnd *K1, p2; rep from * around.
Cont as established until piece measures
2"/5cm from beg.
Next (inc) rnd *K1, p1, M1, p1; rep
from * around—56 sts.
Work 2 rnds more in k1, p1 rib.
Change to B (C, D). Knit one rnd.
Change to larger dpns. Purl 5 rnds.
Next (dec) rnd [P5, p2tog] 8 times
around—48 sts.
Knit 2 rnds.
Next (dec) rnd [K6, k2tog] 6 times
around.
Rep dec rnd every other rnd 3 times more,
working 1 less st before each dec.
Rep dec rnd every rnd in this way until 6
sts rem. Cut yarn, draw tail through open
sts twice.

FINISHING
Weave in ends. Sew button embellishment
to center of cupcake top.
Stuff carefully to create desired cupcake
shape, allowing first 3 ribbed rnds to fold
to center.
Cut a circle with a 2"/5cm diameter out of
cardboard and fit into base of cupcake
under folded edge of rib. ✄

Summer Seaside Pillows

Display these maritime code pillows on the porch for your Independence Day gathering, or use them all year round as fun nautical-themed décor.

Designed by Rebecca Klassen

KNITTED MEASUREMENTS
Approx 15"/38cm x 15.5"/39cm

MATERIALS
- 7 3½oz/100g skeins (each approx 220yd/200m) of Universal Yarn *Deluxe Worsted* (100% wool) in #12257 pulp (A)

- 2 skeins in #12276 twilight (B)

- 1 skein in #12295 red rose (C)

- Size 6 (4mm) circular needle, 24"/60cm long, OR SIZE TO OBTAIN GAUGE

- 3 16" pillow forms (1 for each pillow)

- 9 1" diameter wooden buttons (3 for each pillow)

- Tapestry needle

- Sewing needle and thread

GAUGE
16 sts and 22 rows = 4"/10cm over St st using size 6 (4mm) needles.
TAKE TIME TO CHECK GAUGE.

NOTE The following yarn amounts are needed for each pillow: for Whiskey pillow, 2 skeins A, 1 skein B, 1 skein C; for X-ray pillow, 3 skeins A, 1 skein B; for Victor pillow, 3 skeins A, 1 skein C.

K2, P2 RIB
(multiple of 4 sts plus 2)
Row 1 *K2, p2, rep from * to last 2 sts, k2.
Row 2 *P2, k2, rep from * to last 2 sts, p2.
Rep rows 1 and 2 for k2, p2 rib.

2-STITCH BUTTONHOLE
K2, slip first st over second, k1, slip previous st over third st.

WHISKEY PILLOW FRONT
With B, cast on 62 sts. Work 18 rows in St st.
Row 19 With B, k13; with A, k36; with B, k13.
Work in St st as est for 16 rows more.
Row 36 With B, k13; with A, k12; with C, k12; with A, k12; with B, k13.
Work as est for 16 rows more.
Row 53 With B, k13; with A, k36; with B, k13.
Work as est for 16 rows more. Break A and C. With B, work 18 rows in St st. Bind off on WS.

X-RAY PILLOW FRONT
With A, cast on 24 sts; with B, cast on 14 sts; with A, cast on 24 sts. Work 34 rows in St st as est. Break A. With B, work 19 rows in St st.
Row 54 With A, k24; with B, k14; with A, k24.
Work in St st as est for 33 rows more. Bind off on WS.

VICTOR PILLOW FRONT
Work chart.

BACK TOP (for all three pillows)
With A, cast on 62 sts. Work 28 rows in St st.

BUTTONHOLE BAND
Rows 1 and 2 Work in k2, p2 rib.
Row 3 [K2, p2] 3 times, k2, work 2-st buttonhole, k1, [p2, k2] 3 times, work 2-st buttonhole, k1, [p2, k2] 3 times, sl 2 sts, k1, [p2, k2] 3 times.
Row 4 [P2, k2] 3 times, p2, cast on 2 sts, [p2, k2] 3 times, p2, cast on 2 sts, [p2, k2] 3 times, p2, cast on 2 sts, [p2, k2] 3 times, p2.
Row 5 [K2, p2] 3 times, k2, k2 tbl, [k2, p2] 3 times, k2, k2 tbl, [k2, p2] 3 times, k2, k2 tbl, [k2, p2] 3 times, k2.
Bind off in rib.

BACK BOTTOM
With A, cast on 62 sts. Work 54 rows in St st.

BUTTON BAND
Work 5 rows in k2, p2 rib. Bind off in rib on WS.

FINISHING
Weave in ends. Block pieces. Using mattress stitch, sew outside edges of front to back bottom, then sew outside edges of back top to front, so that ribbed band overlaps that of back bottom. Block additionally as desired. Sew on buttons.

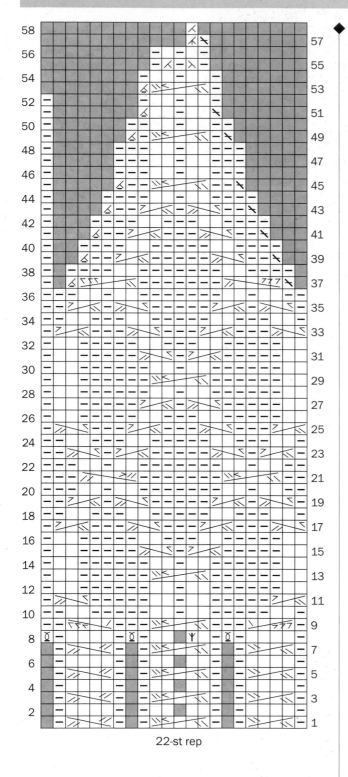

22-st rep

STITCH KEY

Note: At end of rnd 56, move marker 1 st to right.

☐	Knit
⊟	Purl
▨	No stitch
⟋	Ssk
⟍	K2tog
⟰	K3tog
Ɏ	Double inc
⚇	M1P
⟍	P2tog tbl
⟋	P2tog
⟋	3-st RPC
⟋	3-st LPC
⟋	4-st RC
⟋	4-st LC
⟍	4-st RPC
⟋	4-st LPC
⟋	5-st RC
⟋	5-st LC
⟍	5-st RPC
⟋	5-st LPC

HEEL GUSSET

Beg working in the rnd and resume color stripe pat as established.

Work across heel sts. Pick up and k 12 sts along the side of the heel. Pick up a stitch from the row below the first instep st to prevent a hole. Work across 26 instep sts. Pick up 1 st from the row below the first heel st to prevent a hole. Pick up and k 12 sts along the second side of the heel. Work across 26 instep sts. Pm for beg of rnd—66 sts.

Rnd 1 K1, ssk, work to 3 sts from end of sole sts, k2tog, k1. Work across instep.

Rnd 2 Work even.

Repeat rnds 1 and 2 until there are 52 sts remaining.

FOOT

Cont working in rnds until foot measures 9½"/24cm from base of heel, ending with rnd 2 of stripe pat.

SHAPE TOE

Cont with A only.

Rnd 1 Sole: K1, ssk, work to last 3 sts, k2tog, k1. Instep: K1, ssk, work to last 3 sts, k2tog, k1.

Rnd 2 Work even.

Rep rnds 1 and 2 until 32 total sts rem. Rep rnd 1 only until 12 sts remain.

FINISHING

Place 6 instep sts on one needle and 6 sole sts on second needle. With WS together, graft sts tog using kitchener stitch. Weave in ends. 🎀

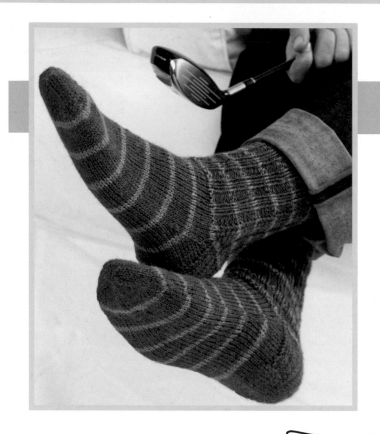

COLOR AND STITCH KEY

⬛	Knit in A
⬜	Knit in B
⧄	3-st RC
⧅	3-st LC

6 sts

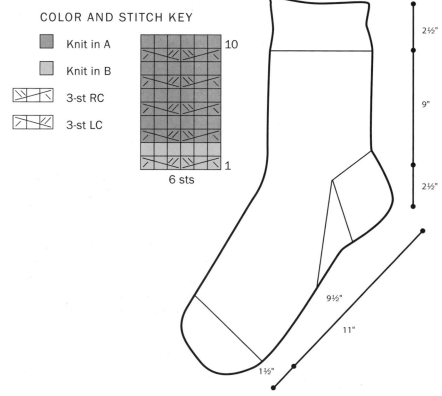

2½"

9"

2½"

9½"

11"

1½"

VICTOR PILLOW FRONT CHART

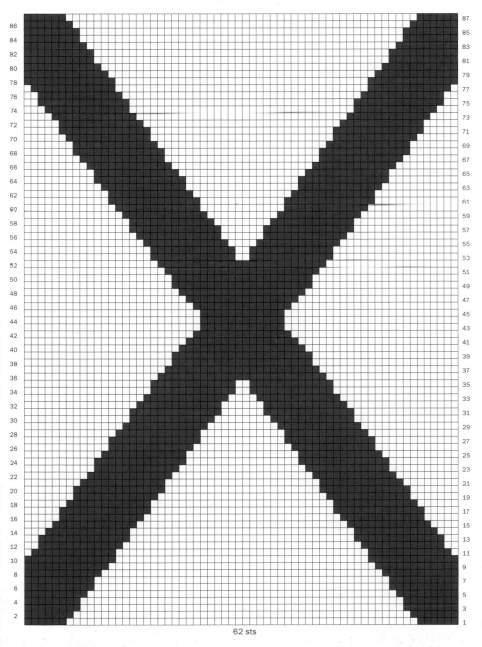

62 sts

COLOR AND STITCH KEY

☐ Knit in A

■ Knit in B

Star Spangled Bunting

Add some red, white, and blue spirit to your Fourth of July celebration with these quick-to-knit stranded stars and flags.

Designed by Stephanie Mrse

KNITTED MEASUREMENTS
Stars 3"/7.5cm across
Triangles 3¾" x 4¼"/9.5cm x 11cm

MATERIALS
■ 1 3½oz/100g skein (each approx 220yd/200m) of Universal Yarn *Deluxe Worsted* (100% wool) each in #12295 red rose (A), #12257 pulp (B), and #3677 cobalt (C)

■ One pair size 7 (4.5mm) needles OR SIZE TO OBTAIN GAUGE

■ One set (5) size 7 (4.5mm) double-pointed needles (dpns)

■ Size G/6 (4mm) crochet hook

GAUGES
20 sts and 26 rows = 4"/10cm over St st using size 7 (4.5mm) needles.
20 sts and 40 rows = 4"/10cm over garter st using size 7 (4.25mm) needles.
TAKE TIME TO CHECK GAUGES.

STITCH GLOSSARY
Dcd Sl 2 sts knitwise, k1, sl 2 slipped sts over k st.

STARS (MAKE 3 EACH IN A, B, AND C)
With dpns, cast on 65 sts and join, being careful not to twist.
Row 1 K5, *dcd, k10; rep from * to last 8 sts, dcd, k5.
Row 2 K4, *dcd, k8; rep from start to last 7 sts, dcd, k4.
Row 3 K3, *dcd, k6; rep from * to last 6 sts, dcd, k3.
Row 4 K2, *dcd, k4; rep from * to last 5 sts, dcd, k1.
Row 5 K1, *dcd, k2; rep from * to last 4 sts, dcd, k1.
Row 6 Dcd 5 times.
Bind off.

ASSEMBLE STAR BUNTING
With crochet hook and A, ch 35. Attach star with a sl st through one point of a star (A). Ch 25. Repeat across with stars in B-C-A-B-C-A-B-C. Ch 35.

TRIANGLES (MAKE 3 EACH IN A, B, AND C)
With straight needles, cast on 20 sts.
Rows 1–3 Knit.
Rows 4–5 K1, k2tog, knit to end.
Rows 6–8 Rep row 1.
Rows 9–10 Rep row 4.
Cont in this manner until 4 sts rem.

Next row K1, k2tog, k1.
Next row Sl 2 knitwise, k1, Bind off.

ASSEMBLE TRIANGLE BUNTING
With crochet hook and B, ch 30. Sl st across the short edge of one triangle (A). Ch 15. Rep across with triangles in B-C-A-B-C-A-B-C. Ch 15.

FINISHING
Weave in ends. Block gently. 🪰

Sunny Day Picnic Blanket

Bring this cheery blanket along on a warm-weather outing with friends and family. Crochet chain stitches help form the bright plaid motif.

Designed by Wilma Peers

KNITTED MEASUREMENTS
Width approx 48"/122cm
Length approx 50"/127cm

MATERIALS
- 3 3½oz/100g skeins (each approx 220yd/200m) of Universal Yarn *Deluxe Worsted* (100% wool) in #12284 strip light yellow (MC)

- 2 skeins each in #12287 cerise (A), #12292 honeysuckle (B), and #61633 greenery (C)

- Size 9 (5.5mm) circular needle, 29"/74cm long, OR SIZE TO OBTAIN GAUGE

- Size G/6 (4mm) crochet hook

- Tapestry needle

GAUGE
16 sts and 21 rows = 4"/10cm over pat st using size 9 (5.5mm) needles.
TAKE TIME TO CHECK GAUGE.

PATTERN STITCH
(multiple of 18 sts plus 13)
Row 1 (RS) K6, p1, *k6, p5, k6, p1; rep from * to last 6 sts, end k6.
Row 2 (WS) P6, k1, *p6, k5, p6, k1; rep from * to last 6 sts, end p6.
Rep rows 1–2 for pat st.

BLANKET
With MC, cast on 193 sts. Work back and forth on circular needle.

COLOR BLOCK STRIPES
*Beg pat st and work for 10 rows. Change to B and work 10 rows. Change to C and work for 10 rows.

PLAID STRIPE
With A, knit 1 row, with MC, purl 1 row, with A, knit 1 row, with MC, purl 1 row, with A, knit 1 row.
Rep from * 6 times more, then work 1 more set of color block stripes.
Note Alternate starting color block stripe sections with a WS then a RS row.
Bind off.

FINISHING THE PLAID
With RS facing and crochet hook, ch st into each row of every p5 rep of the pat. Work colors in A, MC, A, MC, A.

FINISHING
Worked on both side edges: With MC, using the natural roll of St st, roll over and tack down to the adjoining purl row. Worked on cast-on and bind-off edges: With 2 strands of B held tog, pick up one st into every st. Bind off. Weave in ends. ✸

Back-to-School Pencil Case

Give your favorite student a cool place to put tools, with a sporty stripe and fabric lining. Make one for yourself to hold your notions.

Designed by Stephanie Mrse

KNITTED MEASUREMENTS
Width 8½"/21.5cm
Height 5½"/14cm

MATERIALS
■ 1 3½oz/100g skein (each approx 220 yd/201m) of Universal Yarn *Deluxe Worsted* (100% wool) each in #3691 Christmas red (A), #3677 cobalt (B), and #51738 carrot (C)

■ One pair size 5 (3.75mm) needles OR SIZE TO OBTAIN GAUGE

■ 8"/20.3cm zipper

■ 2 pieces of quilter's cotton fabric, approx 9" x 6" (23cm x 15cm) each

■ Sewing needle and thread

GAUGE
20 sts and 28 rows = 4"/10cm over St st using size 5 (3.75mm) needles. *TAKE TIME TO CHECK GAUGE.*

PENCIL CASE
With A, cast on 47 sts.
Work in St st for 2"/5cm, ending on a WS row. Switch to B and, cont in St st, work 2 rows. Switch to C and work 6 rows. Switch to B and work 2 rows. Switch to A and work even for 4"/10cm. Switch to B and work 2 rows. Switch to C and work 6 rows. Switch to B and work 2 rows. Switch to A and work even for 2"/5cm. Bind off.

FINISHING
Weave in ends. Block piece. Fold in half with short sides together. Seam sides of knit case using yarn. Sew zipper to long edges of fabric pieces, right sides together. Sew remaining sides of fabric lining (right sides together) with a ¼"/0.6cm seam. Sew lining and zipper into pencil case. ✄

Campus Cool Cabled Hat

Get ready for the chill of autumn with this versatile topper, knit in striking chevron cables that gradually decrease in size from brim to crown.

Designed by Ashley Rao

KNITTED MEASUREMENTS
Brim circumference 21"/53.5cm
Height 8½"/21.5cm

MATERIALS
■ 2 3½oz/100g skeins (each approx 220yd/201m) of Universal Yarn *Deluxe Worsted* (100% wool) in #12506 azure heather

■ Size 6 (4mm) circular needle, 16"/41cm long, OR SIZE TO OBTAIN GAUGE

■ One set (5) size 6 (4mm) double-pointed needles (dpns)

■ Size 4 (3.5mm) circular needle, 16"/41cm long

■ Cable needle (cn)

■ Waste yarn

■ Stitch marker

GAUGES
18 sts and 24 rnds = 4"/10cm over St st using size 6 (4mm) needle.
26 sts and 26 rnds = 4"/10cm over chevron cable pat using size 6 (4mm) needle.
TAKE TIME TO CHECK GAUGES.

NOTE
This hat is knit from the bottom up, in the round. To create the crown shaping, the cable pattern is decreased from a three-stitch cable crossover to a two-stitch, then to a single stitch. The cable pattern ultimately disappears into paired double decreases.

CHEVRON CABLE PATTERN
(multiple of 12 sts)
Rnd 1 *Sl 3 sts to cn, hold to *back*, k3, k3 from cn, sl 3 sts to cn, hold to *front*, k3, k3 from cn; rep from * around.
Rnds 2–8 Knit.
Rep rnds 1–8 for chevron cable pat.

HAT
Using larger circular needle, cast on 96 sts, pm, and join to work in the rnd, being careful not to twist sts.
Rnds 1–2 Knit.
Rnd 3 * M1, k6, M1, k2; rep from * around—120 sts.
Rnd 4 Knit.
Rnd 5 *M1, k6, M1, k4; rep from * around—144 sts.
Rnd 6 Knit.
Work rnds 1–8 of chevron cable pat 4 times, until hat measures approx 5"/12.5cm from cast-on edge.

Focus on school
and stay warm!

CROWN SHAPING

Note Change to dpns when sts no longer fit comfortably on circular needle.

Rnd 1 *Sl 3 sts to cn, hold to *back*, k3, k3 from cn, sl 3 sts to cn, hold to *front*, k3, k3 from cn; rep from * around.

Rnd 2 Knit.

Rnd 3 *K2tog, k8, ssk; rep from * around—120 sts.

Rnd 4 Knit.

Rnd 5 *K2tog, k6, ssk; rep from * around—96 sts.

Rnd 6 Knit.

Rnd 7 *Sl 2 sts to cn, hold to *back*, k2, k2 from cn, sl 2 sts to cn, hold to *front*, k2, k2 from cn; rep from * around.

Rnd 8 Knit.

Rnd 9 *K2tog, k4, ssk; rep from * around—72 sts.

Rnd 10 *K2tog, k2, ssk; rep from * around—48 sts.

Rnd 11 *Sl 1 st to cn, hold to *back*, k1, k1 from cn, sl 1 st to cn, hold to *front*, k1, k1 from cn; rep from * around.

Rnd 12 Knit.

Rnd 13 *K2tog, k8, ssk; rep from * around—40 sts.

Rnd 14 Knit.

Rnd 15 *K2tog, k6, ssk; rep from * around—32 sts.

Rnd 16 Knit.

Rnd 17 *K2tog, k4, ssk; rep from * around—24 sts.

Rnd 18 Knit.

Rnd 19 *K2tog, k2, ssk; rep from * around—16 sts.

Rnd 20 Knit.

Rnd 21 *K2tog, ssk; rep from * around—8 sts.

Break yarn and draw through rem sts to form a loop. Tighten.

FINISHING

Using smaller needle, pick up each st (96 sts total) from bottom edge. Join yarn, pm and purl one rnd to create a garter st turning ridge. Knit 1"/2.5cm. Break yarn, leaving a 36"/91.5cm tail. Place all sts on waste yarn. Fold facing under. Using tapestry needle and yarn tail sew each st down. Be careful to align 8 facing sts with each 12-st cable panel rep. Adjust tension, remove waste yarn, and weave in loose ends. ❧

Felted Fall Backpack

Autumn colors and sturdy felting make this generous-sized backpack, knit in self-striping yarn, a winner on any campus.

Designed by Erica Schlueter

KNITTED MEASUREMENTS
Approx 15½" x 15½"/39.5cm x 39.5cm after felting

MATERIALS
■ 5 3½oz/100g skeins (each approx 220yd/201m) of Universal Yarn *Deluxe Worsted Long Print* (100% wool) in #10 harvest

■ Size 7 (4.5mm) circular needle, 24"/61cm long, OR SIZE TO OBTAIN GAUGE

■ One pair size 7 (4.5mm) needles

■ Two size 7 (4.5mm) double-pointed needles (dpns)

■ Stitch markers

■ Stitch holder

■ Wide strip of plastic, approx 70"/177.5cm long

GAUGE
16 sts and 22 rows = 4"/10cm in St st using size 7 (4.5mm) needles.
TAKE TIME TO CHECK GAUGE.

BACKPACK
CASING
Using straight needles, cast on 102 sts. Beg St st and work 8 rows. Knit 3 rows. Beg with a WS row, work in St st for 8 more rows, end on RS.

JOIN CASING
With RS facing, pick up 102 sts from cast-on edge with circular needle. Fold up cast-on edge with WS together so the circular needle is in front of the straight needle. With other end of circular needle, purl 2 sts tog, one from back needle and one from front (enter stitch on back needle first). Continue across the row. Cut yarn, leaving 6"/15cm-long tail. Place sts on holder.
Make a second casing, but do not cut yarn, turn and knit across 102 sts, place marker, knit across the 102 sts of the first casing, joining the 2 casings tog. Work in St st in the rnd (k all rnds) until piece measures 29½"/75cm.
Turn work inside out. Distribute 102 sts on each end of the circular needle. Use one of the straight needles and work 3-needle bind-off for the bottom of the bag. Weave in ends.

I-CORD STRAPS (MAKE 2)
With dpns, cast on 3 sts. *K3, do not turn, slide sts to other end of needle. Rep from * until I-cord measures 90"/228.5cm. Bind off.

FINISHING

Cut thick, wide strips of plastic and thread through casing. Tie off plastic strips at the casing opening so they make a continuous loop and won't fall out of casing, so the casing won't felt shut. Turn bag inside out. Place straps in lingerie bag and felt by hand or machine until backpack has shrunk to measurements. Turn bag right side out. After rinsing, place in water so bag and straps are fully covered and add one tablespoon of white vinegar for 10 minutes, rinse. Squeeze gently to get out extra water. Wrap in towel and squeeze to remove more water. Lay flat and let dry.

Take straight needle and push through casing to loosen any felting that may have occurred. Thread 1 strap through both casings in one direction; thread the other strap through both casings starting at the opposite end from the first one. With knitting needle, poke holes at the corners of the bottom of the backpack, push both strap ends through hole in one side, the other straps in holes on the other side. Make overhand knots on strap end inside the bag to secure the straps. Strap lengths can be adjusted by where the knots are tied. 🎀

Dorm Room Throw

Diamonds are formed in the graphic blanket by picking up stitches and then decreasing to form the vertical ridges that bisect each row.

◆

Designed by Diane Zangl

KNITTED MEASUREMENTS
Throw approx
48" x 48"/122cm x 122cm
Diamond width approx 5"/14cm
Diamond height approx 6"/15.5cm

MATERIALS
■ 5 3½oz/100g skeins (each approx 220yd/201m) of Universal Yarn *Deluxe Worsted* (100% wool) in #12192 nitrox blue (MC)

■ 4 skeins in #12502 smoke heather (CC)

■ Size 7 (4.5mm) circular needle, 24"/61cm long, OR SIZE TO OBTAIN GAUGE

■ Stitch markers

GAUGE
18 sts and 36 rows = 4"/10cm over garter st using size 7 (4.5mm) needle.
TAKE TIME TO CHECK GAUGE.

STITCH GLOSSARY
cdd (centered double decrease)
Sl 2 sts tog knitwise to RH needle, knit next st, pass 2 sl sts over knit st.

NOTES
1) When beginning modular diamond, cast on or pick up sts as directed for each row of diamonds.
2) To avoid having to work in cut ends later, catch them as you pick up and knit sts for each new diamond.
3) Slip first st purlwise on all MC end diamonds only. On first diamond of row, sl 1 on all RS rows. On last diamond of row, sl 1 on all WS rows.

MODULAR DIAMOND
(over 49 sts)
Row 1 (WS) Knit to marked center st, p1, k to end of row.
Row 2 Knit to 1 st before marked st, cdd, k to end of row.
Rows 3–46 Rep rows 1–2.
Row 47 K1, p1, k1.
Row 48 Cdd.

THROW
BASE ROW DIAMONDS (MAKE 6)
With MC, cast on 49 sts. Mark center st. Work one rep of modular diamond pattern.

JOIN DIAMONDS
With CC, pick up and k 24 sts along top left edge of 1 MC diamond, M1 and mark as center st, pick up and k 24 sts along top right edge of next MC diamond. Work modular diamond. Rep from * to * 4 times more—5 CC diamonds.

FIRST DIAMOND
**With MC, cast on 24 sts, with RS facing, pick up and k 1 st in last cdd of previous MC row, pick up and k 24 sts along top right edge of first CC diamond in previous row. Work modular diamond.

NEXT FOUR DIAMONDS
With MC and RS facing, pick up and k 24 sts along top left edge of CC diamond in previous row. Pick up center st in last cdd of previous MC row. Pick up and k 24 sts along top right edge of next CC diamond in previous row. Work modular diamond. Rep from * to * 3 times more.

FINAL DIAMOND
With MC and RS facing, pick up and k 24 sts along top left edge of final CC diamond in previous row, 1 st in cdd of previous MC row, cast on 24 sts. Work modular diamond.**
With CC, pick up and k 24 sts along top left edge of MC diamond in previous row. Pick up center st in last cdd of previous CC row. Pick up and k 24 sts along top right edge of next MC diamond in previous row. Work modular diamond. Rep from * to * 4 times more. Rep from ** 3 times more, then from ** to ** once. Weave in ends. 🎀

School Spirit Convertible Mittens

These convenient mittens flip open and secure with a button to free up your fingers. Knit them in your school colors!

Designed by Cheryl Murray

SIZE
Women's Medium

KNITTED MEASUREMENTS
Width 3¾"/9.5cm
Length 10"/25.5cm

MATERIALS
■ 1 3½oz/100g skein (each approx 220yd/201m) of Universal Yarn *Deluxe Worsted* (100% wool) each in #51738 carrot (A) and #3677 cobalt (B)

■ One set size 6 (4mm) double-pointed needlees (dpns) OR SIZE TO OBTAIN GAUGE

■ Size C/2 (2.75mm) crochet hook

■ Waste yarn

■ Stitch markers

■ 6⅞₆" (11mm) buttons

GAUGE
22 sts and 32 rnds = 4"/10cm over St st using size 6 (4mm) needles.
TAKE TIME TO CHECK GAUGE.

RIGHT MITTEN
CUFF
With A, cast on 40 sts.
Divide sts evenly on dpns. Pm and join, being careful not to twist.
Rnd 1 *K2, p2; rep from * to end of rnd.
Rep rnd 1 until piece measures 2½"/6.5cm from cast-on edge.

BODY
With A, work 2 rnds in St st.
Cont in St st, work stripe sequence as foll:
Rnds 1–2 B.
Rnds 3–5 A.
Rnd 6 B.
Rnds 7–9 A.
Rnds 10–11 B.
Rnds 12–15 A.
Rnds 16–17 B.
Rnd 18 A.
Rnds 19–20 B.
Rnds 21–25 A.
AT THE SAME TIME, shape thumb gusset as foll:
Rnd 1 K2, pm, k2, pm, k16, place side marker, knit to end of rnd.
Rnd 2 K2, sl marker, m1, knit to second gusset marker, m1, sl marker, knit to end of rnd.
Rnds 3–4 Work even.
Rep rnds 2–4 until there are 14 sts between gusset markers.
Work even until piece measures 3"/7.5cm from the top of the cuff.
Next rnd Work to first gusset marker, remove marker. Sl 14 sts (gusset sts) to waste yarn, cast on 2 sts. Remove second gusset marker, work to end of rnd—40 sts. Work 2 rnds even.
Next rnd Work to side marker, p20, forming garter ridge (back of hand). Work even until piece measures 3¼"/8cm from the top of the cuff.
Cut A. With B, work k2, p2 rib for 7 rnds. Bind off all sts loosely.

POPOVER
With RS facing, starting at side marker and using A, pick up and k 20 bumps from the garter ridge. With B, cast on 20 sts (palm sts)—40 sts total. Divide sts evenly on dpns and join, being careful not to twist. Place marker.
Rnds 1–7 With B only, k20, *k2, p2; rep from * to end. Change to St st and work stripe sequence as foll:
Rnds 8–10 A.
Rnd 11 B.
Rnds 12–14 A.
Rnds 15–16 B.
Rnds 17–20 A.

POPOVER TOP SHAPING
Rnd 1 With B, k1, ssk, k14, k2tog, k2, ssk, k14, k2tog, k1.
Rnd 2 With B, work even.
Rnd 3 With A, k1, ssk, k12, k2tog, k2, ssk, k12, k2tog, k1.
Rnd 4 With B, work even.

Rnd 5 With B, k1, ssk, k10, k2tog, k2, ssk, k10, k2tog, k1.

Rnd 6 With A, work even.

Rnd 7 With A, k1, ssk, k8, k2tog, k2, ssk, k8, k2tog, k1.

Rnd 9 With A, work even.

Rnd 10 With A, k1, ssk, k6, k2tog, k2, ssk, k6, k2tog, k1.

Rnd 11 With A, work even—24 sts.

Cut yarn, leaving 8"/20.5cm tail. Thread tapestry needle with tail and graft the mitten top using kitchener stitch.

THUMB

Slip the 14 sts on waste yarn to a needle. With A, knit.

Pick up 3 sts from the base of the thumb hole on the hand and pm. Join and distribute evenly on dpns—17 sts. Work in rounds in stripe sequence as foll: 6 rnds A, 7 rnds B, 4 rnds A, 1 rnd B. Change to A.

Next rnd (K4, k2tog) twice, work to end of rnd—15 sts.

Knit 1 rnd even.

Next rnd *K1, k2tog; rep from * around—10 sts.

Next rnd K2tog around—5 sts.

Cut yarn, leaving a tail. Weave tail through remaining stitches.

LEFT MITTEN

Work as for right mitten to thumb gusset, placing side marker after 20th st.

THUMB GUSSET

Rnd 1 Work to last 4 sts before side marker, pm, work 2 sts, pm, complete rnd.

Rnd 2 Work to first gusset marker, sl marker, m1, work to second gusset marker, m1, sl marker, complete rnd.

Rnds 3–4 Work even.

Rep rnds 2–4 until there are 14 sts between gusset markers.

Work even until piece measures 3"/5cm from top of cuff.

BODY

Next rnd Work to first gusset marker, remove gusset marker, sl 14 (gusset sts) to waste yarn, cast on 2 sts, remove second gusset marker, work to end of rnd—40 sts. Work 2 rnds even.

Next rnd Work to side marker, p20, forming garter ridge (back of hand). Work even until piece measures same as right mitten. Cut A. With B work k2, p2 rib for 7 rnds. Bind off all sts loosely.

Foll directions for right mitten popover and thumb.

FINISHING

Weave in ends. Sew 3 buttons onto each mitten, centered on the back at the top of the cuff.

BUTTON LOOPS

With crochet hook and B, make two 7-st chains. Cut yarn and pull through last stitch to fasten. Pull tails through top of each mitten at the center and secure on the inside. 🪰

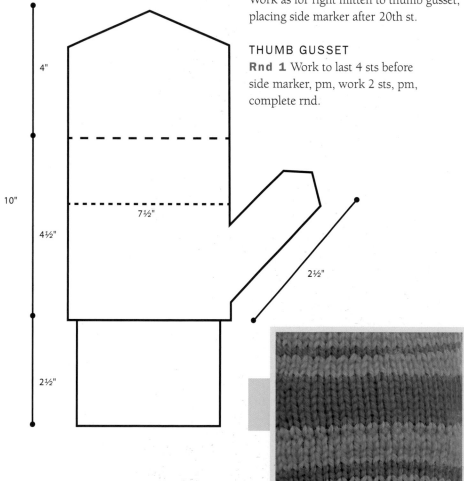

Felted Trick-or-Treat Bag

What's better than a scary jack o' lantern? One that holds candy! This felted bag is great for trick-or-treating, or for storing your own candy to give away.

Designed by Linda Cyr

KNITTED MEASUREMENTS

Height approx 13½"/34.5cm, not including handle (before felting)
Diameter approx 31"/78.5cm at widest point (before felting)
Height approx 9"/23cm, not including handle (after felting)
Diameter approx 12"/30.5cm at widest point (after felting).

MATERIALS

■ 3 3½oz/100g skeins (each approx 220yd/201m) of Universal Yarn *Deluxe Worsted* (100% wool) in #51738 carrot (MC)

■ 2 skeins in #1900 ebony (CC)

■ One pair size 10 (6mm) needles OR SIZE TO OBTAIN GAUGE

■ One set size 10 (6mm) double-pointed needles (dpns)

GAUGE

14 sts and 19 rows = 4"/10cm over St st with yarn held double using size 10 (6mm) needles.
TAKE TIME TO CHECK GAUGE.

NOTES

1) Two strands of yarn are held together throughout, except for trim.
2) When changing colors in intarsia patterns, twist yarns tog to prevent gaps.

STITCH GLOSSARY

cdd (centered double decrease)
Sl 2 sts tog knitwise, k1, psso 2 sl sts.

BAG

With MC and straight needles, cast on 16 sts.
Rows 1 and 2 Sl 1, k across.
Rows 3–10 Sl 1, m1, k across.
Rows 11–22 Sl 1, k across.
Rows 23–29 Sl 1, k2tog, k across.
Row 30 Sl 1, k2tog, k6, pm.
Do not turn, but begin working in the rnd on dpns as foll:
Rnd 1 K8, pick up sts around circumference of piece, 1 st in ea sl st, 1 st for every st along cast-on edge, k8 across last row to get to marker—60 sts.
Rnd 2 [M1, k5] 12 times—72 sts.
Rnds 3 and 4 Knit.
Rnd 5 [M1, k6] 12 times—84 sts.
Rnds 6–8 Knit.
Rnd 9 [M1, k7] 12 times—96 sts.
Rnds 10–13 Knit.
Rnd 14 [M1, k8] 12 times—108 sts.
Rnd 15 Knit.
Beg working back and forth in rows. Cut multiple 1-yd lengths (double strand) of MC and CC. Execute colorwork chart using intarsia technique, adding strands as needed—do not carry non-working yarns.

BEG CHART

Row 1 K41, work row 1 of face chart (26 sts), k41.
Continue in this manner until 28 rows of chart are completed. Continue to work chart over same 26 sts, but begin shaping top as foll:
Row 29 K13, cdd, k22, cdd, k26, cdd, k22, cdd, k13—100 sts.
Rows 30–34 Work even.
Row 35 K12, cdd, k20, cdd, k24, cdd, k20, cdd, k12—92 sts.
Resume working in the round and work 3 rnds even.
Next rnd K11, cdd, k18, cdd, k22, cdd, k18, cdd, k11—84 sts.
Work 3 rnds even.
Next rnd K10, cdd, k16, cdd, k20, cdd, k16, cdd, k10—76 sts.
Work 3 rnds even.
Next rnd K9, cdd, k14, cdd, k18, cdd, k14, cdd, k9—68 sts.
Work 1 rnd even.
Next rnd K8, cdd, k12, cdd, k16, cdd, k12, cdd, k18—72 sts.
Work 1 rnd even.
Bind off all sts. Sew back seam.

TRIM

With 1 strand of CC, cast on 4 sts.

Row 1 Kfb, k1, turn.

Row 2 (and all even-numbered rows) Knit.

Row 3 Kfb, k4, turn.

Row 5 Kfb, k3, turn.

Row 7 Kfb, k6, turn.

Row 9 Ssk, k4, turn.

Row 11 Ssk, k5, turn.

Row 13 Ssk, k2, turn.

Row 15 Ssk, k3, turn.

Row 16 Knit.

Rep rows 1–16 a total of 7 times. Bind off all sts.

CORD

With 2 strands of CC and dpns, cast on 4 sts.

Row 1 K4, do not turn work.

Row 2 Slide sts to other end of needle, bring yarn around back and k4, do not turn.

Rep row 2 until piece measures 42"/107cm long. Cut yarn, thread through all sts.

FINISHING

Weave in ends. Felt by hand or machine. Run more than one cycle if needed to achieve desired result. Stuff bag with crumpled plastic bags to shape, let dry. Using 1 strand of CC, sew trim around top of bag.

APPLY CORD

Attach one end of cord to one side of bag opening, pin cord to bag halfway around to other side, create handle with approx 9"/23cm of cord, pin cord to beginning and then around other side of opening, twist remaining cord around handle, adjust if necessary to fit. Sew cord in place. 🎀

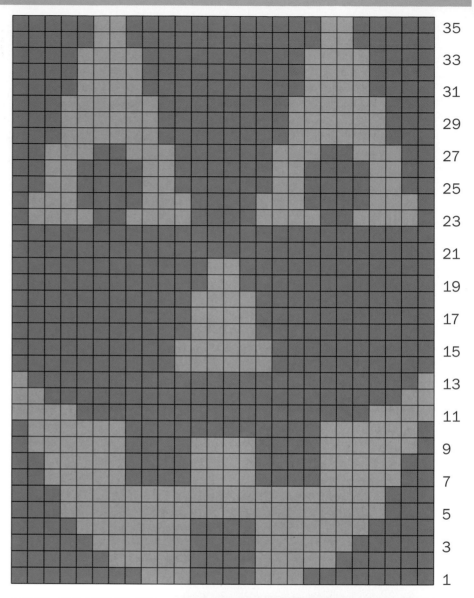

35
33
31
29
27
25
23
21
19
17
15
13
11
9
7
5
3
1

COLOR AND STITCH KEY

■ K on RS, p on WS in MC

■ K on RS, p on WS in CC

Ghoulish Ghost Hat

Ghosts aren't supposed to be this cute! A ruffled brim, tassel, and lopsided grin make for a fun holiday topper, versatile enough to fit adults and kids alike.

Designed by Christina Behnke

KNITTED MEASUREMENTS
Circumference 19¾"/50cm
Height 12"/30.5cm

MATERIALS
■ 1 3½oz/100g skein (each approx 220yd/201m) of Universal Yarn *Deluxe Worsted* (100% wool) each in #12286 lime tree (A) and #1900 ebony (B)

■ One pair size 8 (5mm) needles OR SIZE TO OBTAIN GAUGE

■ Size 8 (5mm) circular needle, 16"/41cm long

■ Stitch markers

■ Tapestry needle

■ Scrap yarn

GAUGE
19 sts and 25 rows = 4"/10cm over St st using size 8 (5mm) needles.
TAKE TIME TO CHECK GAUGE.

NOTES
1) Main portion of hat is worked flat, then joined at the cap with a 3-needle bind-off and seamed. Ruffle is then picked up at bottom edge and worked in the rnd.
2) When changing colors in intarsia pattern, twist yarns tog to prevent gaps.

HAT
With A and straight needles, cast on 92 sts. Work in St st until work measures ½"/1.5cm. On last (WS) row, p41, pm, p10, pm, p to end. Mouth chart will be worked between these two markers over next 10 rows.

MOUTH
Work to marker, sl marker, work row 1 of mouth chart, sl marker, work to end. Rep as established until all rows have been worked. Remove markers. With A, work 4 rows in St st. On last (WS) row, p34, pm, p24, pm, p to end. Eyes chart will be worked between these two markers over next 10 rows.

EYES
Work to marker, sl marker, work row 1 of eyes chart, sl marker, work to end. Cont as established until all rows have been worked. Remove markers. With A, work 4 rows in St st. On last (WS) row, p4, pm, p40, pm, p2, pm, p42, pm, p to end.

DEC ROWS

Row 1 K to 2 sts before marker, ssk, sm, k to 2 sts before marker, k2tog, sm, k2, sm, ssk, k to marker, sm, k2tog, k to end—88 sts.
Row 2 Purl.
Rep rows 1 and 2 until 20 sts remain.

3-NEEDLE BIND-OFF

Divide sts, placing 10 sts each onto a separate piece of scrap yarn. Fold work in half so that WS faces out. Place each set of sts onto a needle, starting from center of work, so that sts at each outside edge of work align with tips of needles. Work each set of sts together in a 3-needle bind-off. Turn work RS out.

FINISHING

Starting at top edge, seam piece together, taking one st from each edge as selvedge st.

RUFFLE

With A and circular needle, and starting at seam with RS facing, pick up and k 90 sts along bottom edge of hat. Join rnd.
Inc row Kfb in every st—180 sts.
Work in St st until ruffle measures 1½"/4cm. Purl 1 row. Bind off loosely in knit. Block to measurements. Weave in ends.

EMBROIDERY

With tapestry needle and B, embroider a running stitch around the ruffle using photo as guide.

TASSEL

Wrap B approx 20 times around a piece of cardboard 5"/12.5cm long. Thread a strand of yarn, insert it in the cardboard and tie it in the top, leaving a long end to tie around the tassel. Cut the lower edge to free the strands. Wrap the long tail tightly several times around the upper edge and insert the ends into the tassel. Trim the strands. Attach to top of hat. 🪰

MOUTH CHART

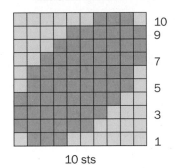

10 sts

COLOR AND STITCH KEY

☐ Knit on RS, p on WS in A
☐ Knit on RS, p on WS in B

EYES CHART

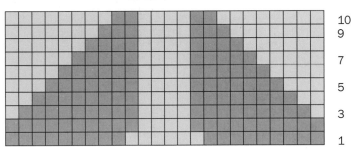

24 sts

Spiderweb Boot Toppers

Need a spooky trick-or-treat accessory? These clever boot toppers feature an embroidered web and a spider that can be adjusted to dangle long or short.

Designed by Amy Micallef

KNITTED MEASUREMENTS
Length approx 11"/28cm
Circumference over ribbing, relaxed approx 10"/25.5cm
Circumference for top approx 17"/43cm

MATERIALS
■ 2 3½oz/100g skeins (each approx 220yd/201m) of Universal Yarn *Deluxe Worsted* (100% wool) in #12256 tangerine flash (MC)

■ 1 skein in #1900 ebony (CC)

■ 1 set (5) each sizes 5 (3.75mm) and 2 (2.75mm) double-pointed needles (dpns) OR SIZE TO OBTAIN GAUGE

■ Tapestry needle

■ Cable needle (cn)

■ Small amount of fiberfill stuffing

■ 2 ⅞"/2.2cm buttons

GAUGE
22 sts and 30 rows = 4"/10cm over St st using size 5 (3.75mm) needles.
TAKE TIME TO CHECK GAUGE.

STITCH GLOSSARY
2-st RPT Sl 1 st to cn, hold to *back*, k1, p1 from cn.

2-st LPT Sl 1 st to cn, hold to *front*, p1, k1 from cn.
3-st RPT Sl 2 sts to cn, hold to *back*, k1, p2 from cn.
3-st LPT Sl 1 st to cn, hold to *front*, p2, k1 from cn.

NOTE
The spider can be lowered and raised, depending on which buttonhole is used.

K2, P2 RIB
(over multiple of 4 sts)
Rnd 1 *K2, p2; rep from * around.
Rep rnd 1 for k2, p2 rib.

BOOT TOPPER (MAKE 2)
With MC, cast on 80 sts. Join in the rnd, being careful not to twist, pm for beg of rnd.

CUFF
Rnds 1–3 Work in k2, p2 rib.
Rnd 4 [K2, p2] 10 times, bind off 2 stitches, p2, [k2, p2] 9 times.
Rnd 5 [K2, p2] 10 times, cast on 2 stitches, p2, [k2, p2] 9 times.
Rnds 6–23 Work in k2, p2 rib.
Rnd 24 Rep rnd 4.
Rnd 25 Rep rnd 5.
Rnds 26–30 Work in k2, p2 rib.
Rnd 31 *K3, M1; rep from * to last 2 sts, k2—106 sts.

FOLDOVER SECTION
Rnds 32–76 P28, work chart, p28.
Rnd 77 *K2, p1, p2tog; rep from * to last 2 sts, k1, p1.
Rnds 78–80 *K2, p2; rep from * to last 2 sts, k1, p1.
Rnd 81 Bind off in pattern.
Weave in ends.

SPIDERWEB
Use CC and tapestry needle to create the spiderweb design. Using the knit sts as a guideline, use an embroidery backstitch to create the radial lines. Add the circular embroidery using the same backstitch technique.

SPIDER
ABDOMEN
With CC and smaller needles, cast on 8 stitches. Join in the rnd, being careful not to twist. Pm at start of rnd.
Rnd 1 Knit.
Rnd 2 *K1, kfb; rep from * to end—12 sts.
Rnd 3 Knit.
Rnd 4 *Kfb, k1; rep from * to end—18 sts.
Rnd 5 Knit.
Rnd 6 *K1, kfb; rep from * to end—27 sts.
Rnds 7–9 Knit.
Rnd 8 *Ssk, k1; rep from * to end—18 sts.
Rnd 9 Knit.
Rnd 10 *K1, ssk; rep from * to end—12 sts.
Rnd 11 Knit.
Rnd 12 *K1, ssk; rep from * to end—8 sts.
Rnd 13 Knit.
Fill abdomen with fiberfill.

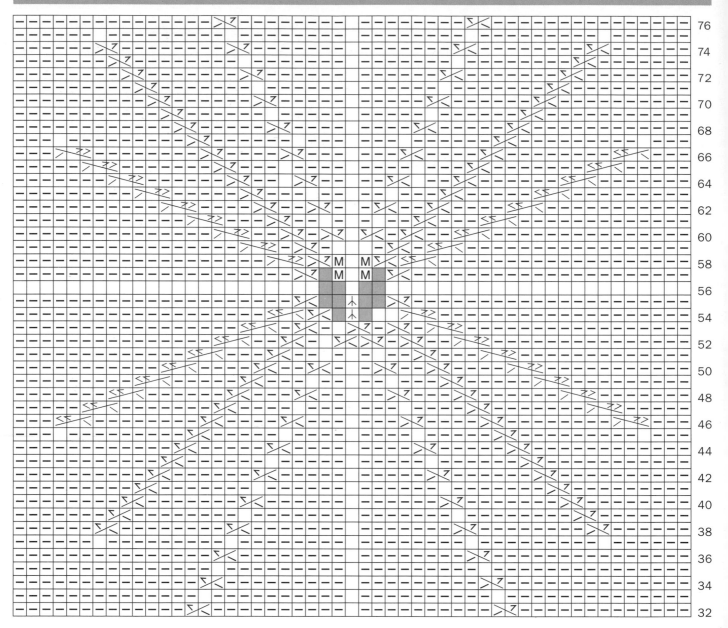

STITCH KEY

☐ Knit	⅄ S2KP	⟋⟍ 2-st LPT	
⊟ Purl	Ⓜ M1	⟍⟋ 3-st RPC	
▨ No stitch	⟍⟋ 2-st RPT	⟋⟍ 3-st LPC	

HEAD

Rnd 14 *K1, kfb; rep from * to end—12 sts.

Rnd 15 Knit.

Rnd 16 *Kfb, k1; rep from * to end—18 sts.

Rnd 17 Knit.

Rnd 18 *K1, ssk; rep from * to end—12 sts.

Rnd 19 Knit.

Rnd 20 *K1, ssk; rep from * to end—8 sts.

Fill head with fiberfill.

Using tapestry needle and a 12"/30.5cm tail, sew through the rem lps and tighten. Tie off.

FINISHING

Run yarn from spider through hole in center of web from front to back. Thread yarn through holes on button and tie securely, adjusting length as necessary. Button can be buttoned through top hole on cuff to let spider dangle, or through bottom hole to attach closely to web.

SPIDER LEGS

With needle and CC, run yarn through spider body and cut off at desired length to make legs. Rep 3 more times for 8 legs total. 🎀

Black Cat Brooch

No costume? Tempt fate and turn heads when you sport this spooky black cat on your lapel. When it's not Halloween, make it in other colors for the cat lovers in your life.

Designed by Lisa Silverman

KNITTED MEASUREMENTS
Length approx 4"/10cm
Height approx 3"/7.5cm

MATERIALS
■ 1 3½oz/100g skein (each approx 220yd/201m) of Universal Yarn *Deluxe Worsted* (100% wool) in #1900 ebony (MC)

■ Small amount in #12288 bashful pink (CC)

■ One set (4) size 4 (3.5mm) double-pointed needles (dpns) OR SIZE TO OBTAIN GAUGE

■ 1½"/3.8cm pin back

■ Fiberfill stuffing

■ Sewing needle and thread

GAUGE
22 sts and 32 rows = 4"/10cm over St st using size 4 (3.5mm) needles.
TAKE TIME TO CHECK GAUGE.

COLOR AND STITCH KEY

■ Duplicate st in CC

■ Duplicate st in MC

BODY (MAKE 2, FOR FRONT AND BACK)

LEFT LEG
Cast on 2 sts.
Row 1 (WS) Purl.
Row 2 Kfb twice—4 sts.
Row 3 and all WS rows Purl.
Row 4 Knit.
Row 6 K1, M1, k2, M1, k1—6 sts.
Row 8 Knit.
Row 10 K1, M1, k4, M1, k1—8 sts.
Row 11 Purl.
Cut yarn, leave sts on holder.

RIGHT LEG
Work as for left through row 11.
Row 12 K8, cast on 1 st, k left leg sts off holder to end.
Rows 13–19 Work even in St st.
Row 20 K1, ssk, knit to last 3 sts, k2tog, k1.
Row 21 P1, ssp, purl to last 3 sts, p2tog, p1.
Rep rows 20–21 twice more. Bind off all sts.

HEAD
Cast on 8 sts.
Row 1 (WS) Purl.
Row 2 K1, M1, k6, M1, k1—10 sts.
Row 3 P1, M1, p8, M1, p1—12 sts.
Rows 4–11 Work even in St st.

BEG EAR SHAPING
Row 12 K5, place these 5 sts on holder for 2nd ear, bind off 2 sts for top of head, k5.
Row 13 P3, p2tog.
Row 14 Ssk, k2.
Row 15 P1, p2tog.
Bind off rem 2 sts. Cut yarn, reattach to work 2nd ear from sts on holder, beg on WS.

Next row Ssp, p3.
Next row K2, k2tog.
Next row Ssp, p1.
Bind off rem 2 sts.

TAIL
Cast on 3 sts. Without turning, slide sts to other end of needle, knit to end. Cont until I-cord measures 5½"/14cm from beg, bind off.

FINISHING
Sew front body to back body around edges, leaving a gap of approx ½"/1.3cm to fill with stuffing. Stuff until firm and sew together.
Sew head to body, using photo as guide. Attach tail at one end and tack down to top of body as in photo to create curve.

EYES
With CC, beginning about one row above center of face, foll chart to create eyes in duplicate stitch. With MC, one stitch from the outside of each eye, work duplicate stitch over half a column of stitches to create line (pupil) in center of eye.

CLAWS
With CC, use straight stitch to embroider three claws at bottom of each foot.

WHISKERS
Cut three 2½"/6.5cm lengths of MC. Thread through face in three consecutive rows just below eyes: 1 length straight across the center row, the 2 other lengths diagonally. Tack down each length with thread, leaving ends loose. Weave in ends. Sew on pin back. ✺

Thanksgiving Throw

Watch the big game wrapped in this cozy throw, which combines cool shades of gray and warm orange in stripes of undulating lace.

Designed by Jacqueline van Dillen

KNITTED MEASUREMENTS
Width approx 41"/105cm
Length approx 55"/140cm

MATERIALS
■ 3 3½oz/100g skeins (each approx 220yd/201m) of Universal Yarn *Deluxe Worsted* (100% wool) each in #12502 smoke heather (A) and #12503 charcoal heather (C)

■ 3 3½oz/100g skeins (each approx 220yd/201m) of Universal Yarn *Deluxe Worsted Long Print* (100% wool) in #06 Hawaiian sunset (B)

■ One pair size 7 (4.5mm) needles OR SIZE TO OBTAIN GAUGE

■ Size G/6 (4mm) crochet hook

GAUGE
18 sts and 28 rows = 4"/10cm in St st using size 7 needles.
TAKE TIME TO CHECK GAUGE.

LACE PATTERN
Row 1 Knit.
Row 2 Purl.
Row 3 K1, *[p2tog] 3 times, [k1, yo] 6 times, [p2tog] 3 times, rep from * until 1 st remains, k1.
Row 4 Purl.
Rep rows 1–4 for lace pat.

NOTES
1) Blanket is worked in three strips, which are then sewn together.
2) Length of strips will increase by about 8" during the sewing process.

BLANKET
1ST STRIP
With A, cast on 80 sts.
*Work in lace pat for 28 rows (7 repeats). Change to B, work in lace pat for 28 rows. Change to C, work in lace pat for 28 rows. Repeat from * 3 times more. Bind off.

2ND AND 3RD STRIPS
Work both as for 1st strip, changing color sequence to C, A, B.

FINISHING
Sew the three strips together lengthwise, with 1st strip in the center. Take care that color changes match up along the edges. Weave in ends and block gently to measurements. 🎀

Autumn Leaves Scarf

Cascading leaves in a trio of autumnal hues make a uniquely shaped scarf that suits the season. Tassels at the ends add a hint of playfulness.

Designed by Nijole Hunter

KNITTED MEASUREMENTS
Width approx 8½"/21.5cm
Length approx 61"/155cm

MATERIALS
■ 1 3½oz/100g skein (each approx 220yd/201m) of Universal Yarn *Deluxe Worsted* (100% wool) each in #41795 nectarine (A), #91467 tulipwood (B), and #12287 cerise (C)

■ One pair size 7 (4.5mm) needles OR SIZE TO OBTAIN GAUGE

GAUGE
19 sts and 28 rows = 4"/10cm over pat st using size 7 (4.5mm) needles.
TAKE TIME TO CHECK GAUGE.

NOTES
1) Sl first st of every row wyif purlwise.
2) Twist yarns at color changes on WS every row to prevent holes.

SCARF
With A, cast on 9 sts.
Row 1 (RS) With A, sl 1, k1, p1, attach B, k3, attach C, p1, k2.
Row 2 (WS) With C, sl 1, p1, k1, with B, p3, with A, k1, p1, k1.
Row 3 With A, sl 1, k1, p1, with B, k1, yo, k1, yo, k1, with C, p1, k2—11 sts.
Row 4 With C, sl 1, p1, k1, with B, p5, with A, k1, p1, k1.
Row 5 With A, sl 1, k1, p1, with B, knit to center st of section B, yo, k1, yo, work to end of section B, with C, p1, k2—13 sts.
Row 6 With C, sl 1, p1, k1, purl color B section, with A, k1, p1, k1.
Rep rows 5 and 6 eight times more—29 sts.

CENTER SECTION
Row 1 (RS) With A, sl 1, yo, k1, yo, p1, with B, SKP, k to last 2 sts of section B, k2tog, with C, p1, yo, k1, yo, k1—31 sts.
Row 2 (WS) With C, sl 1, p3, k1, with B, purl section B, with A, k1, p3, k1.
Row 3 With A, sl 1, k1, yo, k1, yo, k1, p1, with B, SKP, k to last 2 sts of section B, k2tog; with C, p1, k1, yo, k1, yo, k2—33 sts.
Row 4 With C, sl 1, p5, k1, with B, purl section B, with A, k1, p5, k1.
Row 5 With A, sl 1, knit to center st of section A, yo, k1, yo, k to last st of section A, p1, with B, SKP, k to last 2 sts of section B, k2tog, with C, p1, k to center st of section C, yo, k1, yo, k to end—35 sts.

Row 6 With C, sl 1, purl to last st of section C, k1, with B, purl section B, with A, k1, p to last st of section A, k1. Rep rows 5 and 6 seven times more—49 sts.

Row 21 With A, sl 1, k to center st of section A, yo, k1, yo, k to last st of section A, p1, with B, SK2P, with C, p1, k to center st of section C, yo, k1, yo, knit to end—51 sts.

Row 22 With C, sl 1, p to last st of section C, k1, with B, purl section B, with A, k1, p to last st of section A, k1.

Row 23 With A, sl 1, SKP, k to last 3 sts of section A, k2tog, p1, with B, yo, k1, yo, with C, p1, SKP, k to last 3 sts of section C, k2tog, k1—49 sts.

Row 24 With C, sl 1, p to last st of section C, k1, with B, purl section B, with A, k1, p to last st of section A, k1.

Row 25 With A, sl 1, SKP, k to last 3 sts of section A, k2tog, p1, with B, k to center st of section B, yo, k1, yo, k to end of section B, with C, p1, SKP, k to last 3 sts of section C, k2tog, k1—47 sts.

Row 26 With C, sl 1, p to last st of section C, k1, with B, purl section B,

with A, k1, p to last st of section A, k1. Rep rows 25 and 26 eight times more—31 sts.

Row 43 With A, sl 1, SK2P, p1, with B, k10, yo, k1, yo, k10, with C, p1, SK2P, k1—29 sts.

Row 44 With C, sl 1, p1, k1, with B, p23, with A, k1, p1, k1.

Repeat center rows 1–44 six times more.

END SECTION

Row 1 (RS) With A, sl 1, k1, p1, with B, SKP, k to last 2 sts of section B, k2tog, with C, p1, k2—27 sts.

Row 2 (WS) With C, sl 1, p1, k1, with B, purl section B, with A, k1, p1, k1. Rep rows 1 and 2 nine times more—9 sts.

Row 21 With A, sl 1, k8. Bind off.

FINISHING

Make four tassels: 2 color A, 1 color B, 1 color C.

Wind yarn about 20 times around a piece of cardboard 2½"/6.5cm long. Tie the yarn bundle together at one end with separate length of yarn. Cut the yarn from opposite end of the bundle and slide the unfinished tassel from the cardboard. Wind another piece of yarn 2–3 times around bundle, approx 1"/2.5cm below tie. Tie two tassels on each end of the scarf, one to the 2nd st on the right side and one to the 2nd st on the left side.

Weave in ends. Lightly block the scarf to flatten it and accentuate the leaves. 🎀

Harvest Market Bag

Carry groceries from the farmer's market to your Thanksgiving table in style with this graphically patterned tote, with a fabric lining and handy inner pocket.

Designed by Mari Tobita

KNITTED MEASUREMENTS
Width approx 10"/25.5cm
Height (without handles) approx 11½"/29cm

MATERIALS
■ 1 3½oz/100g skein (each approx 220yd/201m) of Universal Yarn *Deluxe Worsted* (100% wool) each in #12174 ginseng (MC) and #91477 red oak (CC)

■ One pair size 7 (4.5mm) needles OR SIZE TO OBTAIN GAUGE

■ One pair size 4 (3.5mm) needles

■ One set (5) size 7 (4.5mm) double-pointed needles (dpns)

■ 1yd/0.91m of ¾"/2cm twill tape

■ 1yd/0.91m lining fabric

■ Sewing needle and thread

GAUGES
21 sts and 28 rows = 4"/10cm over St st using size 7 (4.5mm) needles.
21.5 sts and 23.5 rows = 4"/10cm over chart pat using size 7 (4.5mm) needle.
TAKE TIME TO CHECK GAUGES.

BAG FRONT/BACK (MAKE 2)
With MC and larger straight needles, cast on 55 sts.
Work in St st for 34 rows, always knitting the first and last sts for garter selvedge.

BEG CHART
Work rows 1–42 of chart.
After working final row of chart, cut MC, leaving a 6"/15cm tail.
Knit 2 rows with CC.
Change to smaller needles and work 5 rows St st.
Bind off. Block the 2 pieces to measurements and sew sides and bottom.
Weave in all ends.

HANDLES (MAKE 2)
With CC and dpns, cast on 10 sts.
Divide sts among 3 needles, join to work in the rnd, being careful not to twist sts.
Work in St st (k every row) until piece measures 14"/35.5cm.
Insert twill tape inside of handles, bind off and close ends.

POCKET
Cut a piece of lining fabric 6½"/16.5cm x 6"/15cm. Fold over ½"/1.5cm on 2 short raw edges and 1 long raw edge to WS and pin. Fold ½"/1.5cm of rem long raw edge (top of pocket) to WS twice and pin. Press the pocket. Sew the top of pocket.

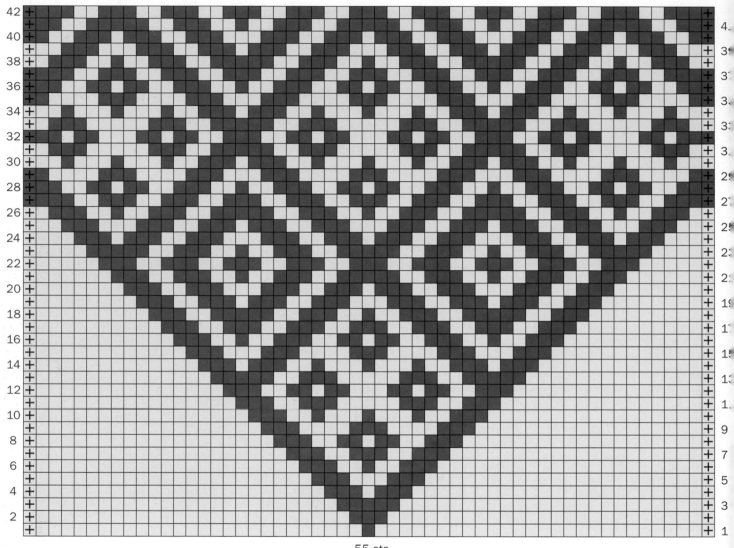

55 sts

LINING

Cut one piece of lining fabric 23"/58.5cm x 11"/28cm. Position the pocket centered 2"/5cm below top of lining. Pin in place, stitch three sides, reinforcing top corners. With RS together (pocket is inside), fold lining in half. Sew ½"/1.5cm seams on sides and bottom. Press seams open. Insert lining into bag, with upper edge aligned with turning row.
Fold knit facing to inside, over lining, and sew in place.

FINISHING

Place handles inside of bag (on top of facing) and 2"/5cm from side seams. Sew in place. ⤫

COLOR AND STITCH KEY

☐ K on RS, p on WS in MC

■ K on RS, p on WS in CC

⊞ K on RS and WS

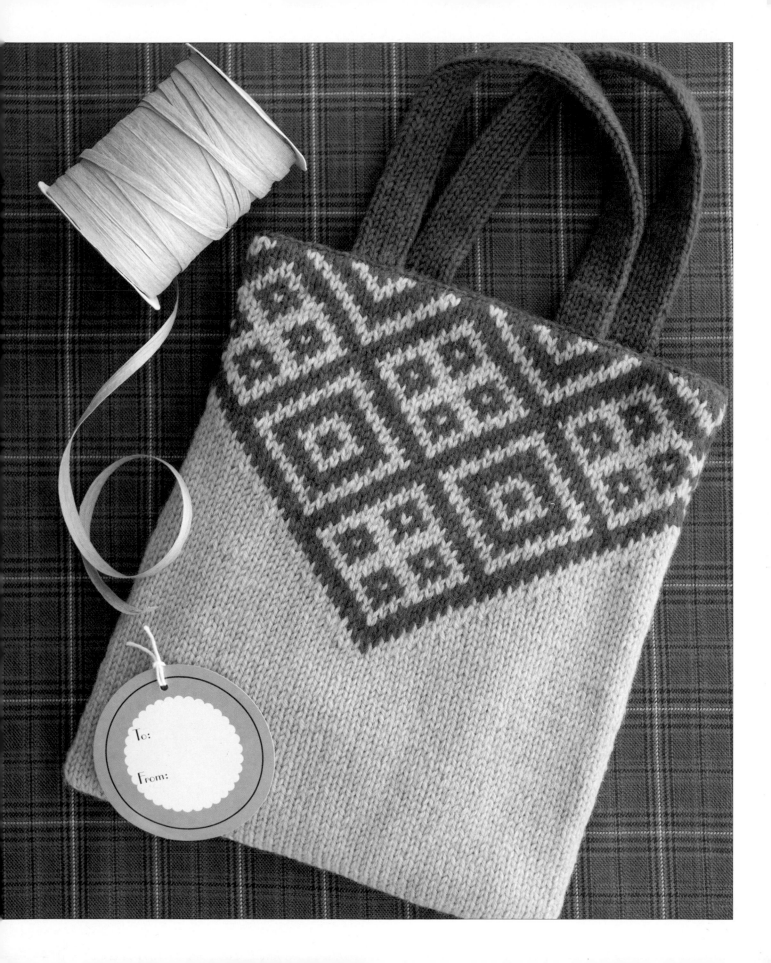

Windy Day Appliqué Scarf

The recipient of this scarf will be giving thanks all winter long. A corded edging, diagonal stripes, and winding appliqué leaves make it a showstopper.

Designed by Wilma Peers

KNITTED MEASUREMENTS
Width (excluding trim) approx 9"/23cm
Length approx 53"/134.5cm

MATERIALS
■ 1 3½oz/100g skein (each approx 220yd/201m) of Universal Yarn *Deluxe Worsted* (100% wool) each in #12281 clay (A), #12170 madder red (B), and #12174 ginseng (C)

■ 1 3½oz/100g skein (each approx 220yd/201m) of Universal Yarn *Renew Wool* (65% virgin wool/35% repurposed wool) in #106 lichen (D)

■ One pair size 10½ (6.5mm) needles OR SIZE TO OBTAIN GAUGE

■ One set (4) size 9 (5.5mm) double-pointed needles (dpns)

■ Tapestry needle

■ Waste yarn or stitch holder

GAUGE
20 sts and 32 rows = 4"/10cm in garter st using size 10½ (6.5mm) needles.
TAKE TIME TO CHECK GAUGE.

NOTE
Scarf is worked in three panels and seamed together. Edging is worked separately and sewn on.

I-CORD
Cast on 4 sts to a single dpn. Knit across. *Slide stitches to right side of needle and, bringing yarn behind, k across row. Repeat from * until desired length.

SCARF
TRIANGLE PANELS
(MAKE 2, ONE EACH IN A AND B)
With larger needles, cast on 2 sts.
Rows 1–13 Knit.
Row 14 K1, m1, k to end.
Repeat rows 1–14 until straight side measures 53". Bind off.

CENTER PANEL
With larger needles and C, cast on 8 sts. Knit every row until length matches straight edge of triangle panels.
Stitch long side of center panel to straight sides of each triangle panel, using the edge bumps of the garter ridges.

EDGING
With D and dpn, cast on 4 sts.
Work I-cord for 4"/10cm. Cut yarn and place I-cord on waste yarn or stitch holder. Repeat until there are enough cords to form edging—approx 105. Do not cut yarn on last I-cord.
Slide I-cord to right side of needle, place sts from next I-cord to left of 1st I-cord, k across 8 sts, binding off at same time. *Pick up sts from end of first I-cord, looping behind second I-cord, and k across, binding off. Place sts from next I-cord on needle to right of last st. K across, binding off. Rep from * until edging is long enough to go around sides of scarf.

APPLIQUÉ
With dpns and D, cast on 3 sts.
Work I-cord for approx 8".

LEAVES
With size 6 needles and D, cast on 3 sts.
Row 1 and all odd-numbered rows Purl.
Row 2 (RS) K1, yo, k1, yo, k1.
Row 4 K2, yo, k1, yo, k2.
Row 6 K1, m1, k2, yo, k1, yo, k2, m1, k1.
Row 8 K1, m1, k3, yo, k1, yo, k3, m1, k1.
Row 10 K1, ssk, k2, yo, k1, yo, k2, k2tog, k1.
Row 12 Rep row 10.
Row 14 K1, sssk, k1, yo, k1, yo, k1, k3tog, k1.
Row 16 K1, sssk, yo, k1, yo, k3tog, k1.
Row 18 Sssk, yo, k1, yo, k3tog.
Row 20 Sssk, k2tog.
Bind off rem 2 sts.

FINISHING
Sew on I-cord vine and leaves, using photo as guide. Sew on edging. Weave in all ends. Block lightly to measurements. 🪰

Acorn Placecards

Keep your Thanksgiving table organized and your guests impressed when you attach these sweet acorns to placecards. Personalize them in different seasonal colors.

Designed by Vanessa Putt

KNITTED MEASUREMENTS
Height approx 2"/5cm
Diameter approx 1"/2.5cm

MATERIALS
■ 1 3½oz/100g skein (each approx 220yd/200m) of Universal Yarn *Deluxe Worsted* (100% wool) each in #12174 ginseng (A), #12181 bronze brown (B), and #12179 dark oak (C)

■ One set (4) size 3 (3.25mm) double-pointed needles (dpns) OR SIZE TO OBTAIN GAUGE

■ Polyester fiberfill

■ Placecards with holes (optional)

GAUGE
22 sts and 32 rows = 4"/10cm over St st using size 3 (3.25mm) needles.
TAKE TIME TO CHECK GAUGE.

NOTE
Acorns can be worked in any combination of colors A, B, and C. Work one with A as the base and B as the cap, and another with B as the base and C as the cap.

ACORN
With A, cast on 4 sts.
Row 1 Kfb around—8 sts.
Row 2 Knit.
Row 3 K1, m1, *k2, m1, rep from * twice more—12 sts.
Row 4 Knit.
Row 5 *K2, m1, rep from * around—18 sts.
Rows 6–11 Knit. Drop A, switch to C.

CAP
Row 12 With C, knit.
Rows 13–14 Purl.
Row 15 *P2tog, p1, rep from * around—12 sts.
Row 16 Purl.
Stuff acorn with polyester fiberfill until firm.
Row 17 P2tog around—6 sts.
Row 18 Purl.
Row 19 P2tog around—3 sts.
Row 20 Finish by slipping sts onto 1 dpn. Slip 1, p2tog, psso. Fasten off, leaving a long tail.

FINISHING
Weave in ends. Use long tail to attach acorns to placecards, if desired. 🦋

Felted Casserole Carrier

Bring your favorite side dish to Thanksgiving dinner in this sturdy felted carrier, or simply make it as a heartwarming hostess gift.

Designed by Loretta Dachman

KNITTED MEASUREMENTS
Carrier 12"/30.5cm wide x 32"/81.3cm long
Cross piece 8"/20.3cm wide x
36–44"/91.4–111.8cm long (see Note 4)

MATERIALS
- 2 3½oz/100g skeins (each approx 220yd/201m) of Universal Yarn *Deluxe Worsted Concord Tweed* (90% wool/7% acrylic/3% viscose) in #903 rojo (B)

- 1 skein each in #905 gold spice (A) and #907 eggplant (C)

- Two size 8 (5mm) circular needles, each 24"/60cm long, OR SIZE TO OBTAIN GAUGE

- Two size 8 (5mm) double-pointed needles (dpns)

- Two ½"/1.3cm dowels, each 12"/30.5 long

- Four 18mm magnetic buttons

GAUGES
30 sts and 31 rows over garter st =
7" x 4" (unfelted) and 6¼" x 3½"
(felted, unblocked)

30 sts and 31 rows over slip st pat =
6" x 4"/15.2 x 10.2cm (unfelted) and
5" x 3"/12.7 x 7.6cm (felted, unblocked)
TAKE TIME TO CHECK GAUGES.

NOTES
1) Even though felted fabric has less "give," the carrier should be supported underneath with one hand while the other hand is holding the handles.
2) Carrier may be lined to reinforce.
3) The carrier front and back are each knit on separate circular needles so that either A or C can be used for 3-needle bind-off. Yarns A and C are at opposite ends when RS are together.
4) The cross piece should felt to 36"/91.4cm long. It can be blocked up to 44"/111.8cm long, depending on amount of overlap desired. Carrier shown has cross piece blocked to 44"/111.8cm.
5) Slip stitch pattern may be worked from chart or text.

3-NEEDLE BIND-OFF
1) Hold right sides of pieces together on two needles. Insert third needle knitwise into first st of each needle, and wrap yarn knitwise.
2) Knit these two sts together, and slip them off the needles. *Knit the next two sts together in the same manner.
3) Slip first st on 3rd needle over 2nd st and off needle. Rep from * in step 2 across row until all sts are bound off.

MACHINE FELTING
1) Use a low water setting and hottest temperature in a top-loading washing machine. Add small amount of laundry detergent and jeans or towels for agitation.
2) Place item in a lingerie bag or zippered pillowcase and add to machine. Check the felting progress frequently, removing item when the individual stitches are no longer visible and item is felted to the desired size.
3) Place item in cool water to stop the felting process and remove suds. Remove from lingerie bag and roll gently in towel to remove excess water.
4) Block and shape while wet. Pin into shape or stuff with plastic bags, and allow to air dry completely.

SLIP STITCH PAT
(multiple of 4 sts plus 2)
Row 1 (WS) With A, purl.
Row 2 With B, k1, sl 1 wyib, *k2, sl 2 wyib; rep from *; end k2, sl 1, k1.
Row 3 With B, p1, sl 1 wyif, *p2, sl 2 wyif; rep from *; end p2, sl 1, p1.
Row 4 With A, knit.
Row 5 With C, p2, *sl 2 wyif, p2; rep from *.
Row 6 With C, k2, * sl 2 wyib, k2; rep from *.

CARRIER FRONT
HANDLE LOOPS (MAKE 2)
With A and size 8 (5mm) needles, cast on 30 sts.

BEG SLIP STITCH PAT
Work 6-row repeat of pat 7 times.
Cut all yarns.
Move 15 sts to each dpn and fold lengthwise with RS together. Sew cast-on edge together. Turn RS out and set aside.

BODY

With C, cast on 44 sts. Cut yarn and set aside.

Next row (WS) With fold of first handle loop on the right, join A, [purl 1 st from front dpn tog with 1 st from back dpn] 15 times, purl 44 cast-on sts, with fold of 2nd handle loop on the left, [purl 1 st from front dpn tog with 1 st from back dpn] 15 times—74 sts. Work 6-row repeat of chart 20 times. Work row 1 of chart. Cut yarn and set aside.

CARRIER BACK

Work same as front but do not cut yarn. Join front and back pieces using 3-needle bind-off.

CROSS PIECE

With C and size 8 (5mm) needles, cast on 39 sts.

Work in garter st (k every row) until 41"/104.1cm long. Bind off.

FINISHING

Weave in all ends. Machine felt both pieces.
Block pieces to measurements (see Note 4).
With carrier WS facing, place cross piece over center carrier. Attach carrier to cross piece by sewing along 3 sides to create a pocket for cold/hot pack. Insert dowels in handle loops at edge away from carrier body. Sew seams under dowels to hold in place. Place casserole dish on carrier. Overlap cross piece to determine placement of magnetic buttons. Sew buttons in place. 🎀

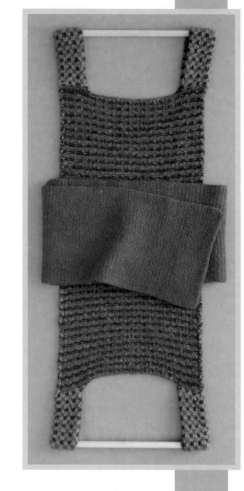

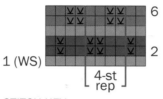

6

2

1 (WS)

4-st rep

STITCH KEY

☐ K on RS, p on WS

☑ Sl 1 wyib on RS, sl 1 wyif on WS

COLOR KEY

■ A (gold spice)

■ B (rojo)

■ C (eggplant)

↑ Direction of work

4"

8"

8"

8"

4"

16" 2" 8" 2" 16"

Hanukkah Hat

The subtle dreidel motif on this Fair Isle cap makes it perfect for the eight days of Hanukkah, and just as wearable all season long.

Designed by Kyle Kunnecke

SIZE
Adult Large

KNITTED MEASUREMENTS
Brim circumference 21"/53.5cm
Height 9"/23cm

MATERIALS
■ 1 3½oz/100g skeins (each approx 220yd/201m) of Universal Yarn *Deluxe Worsted Long Print* (100% wool) in #05 midnight blues (MC)

■ 1 3½oz/100g skein (each approx 220yd/201m) of Universal Yarn *Deluxe Worsted* (100% wool) in #12270 natural (CC)

■ One set each sizes 5 (3.75mm) and 6 (4mm) double-pointed needles (dpns) OR SIZE TO OBTAIN GAUGE

■ Stitch markers

GAUGE
24 sts and 22 rows = 4"/10cm
in St st worked in the rnd using larger needles.
TAKE TIME TO CHECK GAUGE.

K2, P2 RIB
(over multiple of 4 sts)
Rnd 1 *K2, p2; rep from * around.
Rep rnd 1 for k2, p2 rib.

HAT
Using MC and smaller needles, cast on 128 sts.
Work k2, p2 rib for 1½"/4cm.
Next (inc) rnd M1, k74, m1, k to end of round—130 sts. Change to larger needles.
Next rnd Knit.
Work rnds 1–21 of chart, repeating each row 13 times around.
Break off CC, leaving a 6"/15.2cm tail.
Complete hat with MC only.

CROWN SHAPING
Next rnd [K26, pm] 4 times, k26.
Next (dec) rnd [Ssk, k to 2 sts before m, k2tog] 5 times.
Next rnd Knit.
Repeat these two rnds 12 times—10 sts rem.

FINISHING
Cut yarn, leaving an 8"/20cm tail. Weave through rem sts. Pull tog tightly and secure. Weave in all ends. ✿

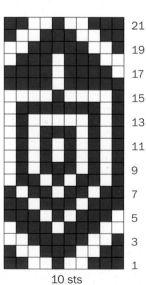

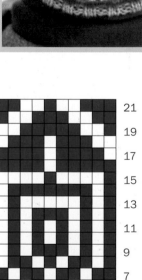

COLOR AND STITCH KEY

■ Knit in MC
□ Knit in CC

21
19
17
15
13
11
9
7
5
3
1

10 sts

Argyle Mitten Garland

Mix and match various colors in this sweet garland of tiny argyle mittens and string up some joy this holiday season.

Designed by Erin Slonaker

KNITTED MEASUREMENTS
Each mitten is approx 2½"/6.5cm wide and 4"/10cm high. Garland is approx 30"/76cm long.

MATERIALS
■ 1 3½oz/100g skein (each approx 220yd/201m of Universal Yarn *Deluxe Worsted Concord Tweed* (90% wool/7% acrylic/3% viscose) each in #907 eggplant, #908 coffee, #903 rojo, #902 aquamarine, and #905 gold spice

■ One set (5) size 7 (4.5mm) double-pointed needles (dpns) OR SIZE TO OBTAIN GAUGE

■ Size G/6 (4mm) crochet hook

■ Stitch markers

■ Tapestry needle

■ Waste yarn

GAUGE
22 sts and 28 rows = 4"/10cm over St st using size 7 (4.5mm) needles.
TAKE TIME TO CHECK GAUGE.

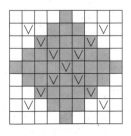

NOTES
1) Each mitten uses three colors: main background (A), diamond (B), and intersecting lines (C).
2) The color C lines are duplicate-stitched after knitting the hand.
3) One skein of each color is enough to make many mittens.
4) Mittens are worked flat; thumb is worked in the round.

STITCH GLOSSARY
M1R With left needle, lift strand between needles from back to front. Knit lifted loop through the front.
M1L With left needle tip, lift strand between needles from front to back. Knit lifted loop through the back.

MITTEN (MAKE 9)
CUFF
With A, cast on 25 sts.
Row 1 (K1, p1) to end, end k1.
Row 2 (P1, k1) to end, end p1.
Rep last two rows 3 more times.

HAND
Row 9 K12, pm, M1R, k1, M1L, pm, k12.
Row 10 Purl. **Row 11** K12, sl marker, M1R, k3, M1L, sl marker, k12. **Row 12** Purl. **Row 13** K12, sl marker, M1R, k5, M1L, sl marker, k12. **Row 14** Purl.
Row 15 K5, join B and k1, join second ball of A and k5, sl thumb sts (sts between markers) onto a holder, removing markers, k to end with A.
Rows 16–22 Cont as established, working rows 2–8 of chart.
Row 23 K1, ssk, k3, with B, k1, with A, k3, k2tog, ssk, k to 3 sts from end, k2tog, k1. **Row 24** Purl. **Row 25** K1, ssk, k5, k2tog, ssk, k to 3 sts from end, k2tog, k1.
Row 26 Purl. **Row 27** K1, ssk, k3, k2tog, ssk, k3, k2tog, k1. **Row 28** P1, p2tog, p1, p2tog tbl, p2tog, p1, p2tog tbl, p1.
Cut yarn, leaving a tail long enough to sew down side seam, draw through rem sts, and pull tight.

THUMB
Set-up rnd With dpns and A, pick up 3 sts along top of thumb opening, then knit to end of rnd. Knit 4 rnds.
Next rnd K2tog around. Cut yarn, draw through rem sts, pull tight.

DUPLICATE STITCH
Foll chart, duplicate st the cross of the argyle using C.

FINISHING
Sew seam of mitten. Weave in ends.

GARLAND
With crochet hook and desired color, ch 30. Sl st into the cuff of one mitten. [Ch 25, sl st into cuff] for rem mittens. Ch 30 and fasten off ends. Secure.

COLOR AND STITCH KEY

☐ K on RS, p on WS in A	▨ K on RS, p on WS	Ⅴ Duplicate stitch in C

Nordic Winter Gloves

Share the holiday spirit with someone you love: the stranded heart pattern on these gloves will keep hands warm from Christmas through Valentine's Day.

Designed by Cheryl Murray

◼◼◼◻◻

SIZE
Woman's Medium

KNITTED MEASUREMENTS
Hand circumference 7½"/19cm

MATERIALS:
◼ 1 3½oz/100g skein (each approx 220yd/201m) of Universal Yarn *Deluxe Worsted* (100% wool) each in #12294 real red (A) and #12257 pulp (B)

◼ One set each sizes 6 (4mm) and 7 (4.5mm) double-pointed needles (dpns) OR SIZE TO OBTAIN GAUGES

◼ Waste yarn

◼ Stitch markers

◼ Tapestry needle

GAUGES
24 sts and 26 rows = 4"/10cm over stranded pat using size 7 (4.5mm) needles.
24 sts and 30 rows = 4"/10cm over St st using size 6 (4mm) needles.
TAKE TIME TO CHECK GAUGES.

NOTE
Gloves are identical for left and right hands.

GLOVES (MAKE 2)
CUFF
With A and smaller dpns, cast on 48 sts. Divide sts evenly on dpns. Join and pm for beg of rnd, being careful not to twist.
Rnd 1 *K2, p2. Rep from * to end of rnd. Rep rnd 1 until piece measures 2½"/6.5cm or desired length from cast-on edge.

BODY AND THUMB GUSSET
Change to larger dpns and work sts 1–24 of chart, pm for side, rep sts 1–24 once more.
Work until rnd 21 of chart is complete, adding sts for thumb gusset as indicated—65 sts.
Next rnd Place 17 sts on holder for thumb. Rejoin and cont working even until chart is complete.

LITTLE FINGER
Next rnd With smaller needles and A only, work to last 6 sts before side marker. Sl 18 sts just worked onto waste yarn. Work next 12 sts. Slip rem 18 sts onto waste yarn. Cast on 2 sts. Arrange the 14 sts on 3 dpns, join, and work in rnds until finger measures 1¾"/4.5cm (or desired length) from base.
Rnd 1 K3, k2tog, k3 sts, k2tog, k4— 12 sts.
Rnd 2 Knit.
Rnd 3 *K1, k2tog; rep from * around— 8 sts.
Cut yarn, leaving a tail. Weave tail through remaining finger stitches.

RING FINGER
Place next 6 sts from front and back waste yarn onto dpns. Reattach yarn and pick up 2 sts from cast-on at base of previous finger. Arrange the 14 sts on 3 dpns, join, work in rnd until finger measures 2½"/6.5cm from base.
Rnd 1 K3, k2tog, k3 sts, k2tog, k4— 12 sts.
Rnd 2 Knit.
Rnd 3 *K1, k2tog; rep from * around— 8 sts.
Cut yarn, leaving a tail. Weave tail through rem finger sts.

MIDDLE FINGER
Work as for ring finger, working in rnd until finger measures 3"/7.5cm before dec.

INDEX FINGER
Work as for ring finger, working in rnd until finger measures 2½"/6.5cm before dec.

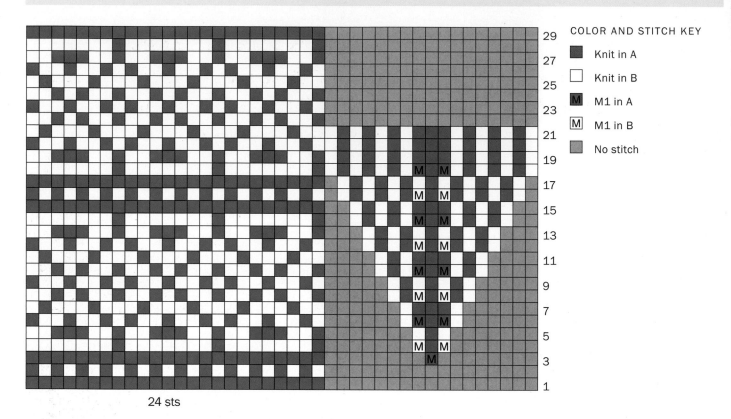

29
27
25
23
21
19
17
15
13
11
9
7
5
3
1

COLOR AND STITCH KEY

■ Knit in A

□ Knit in B

M M1 in A

M M1 in B

No stitch

24 sts

Work two 24-st repeats for each round

THUMB

With smaller dpns, pick up and k 2 sts from the base of the thumb hole on the hand. Knit 17 sts from waste yarn. Join and distribute evenly on needles—19 sts.

Rnd 1 Knit.

Rnd 2 [K6, k2tog] twice, k to end—17 sts.

Work even until thumb measures 1"/2.5cm from base.

Next rnd K7, k2tog, k to end—16 sts.

Work even until thumb measures 1¾"/4.5cm from base.

SHAPE TIP

Rnd 1 *K2, k2tog; rep from * to end—12 sts.

Rnd 2 Knit.

Rnd 3 *K1, k2tog; rep from * to end—8 sts.

Cut yarn, leaving a tail. Weave tail through rem sts.

FINISHING

Use yarn tails to close any holes at bases of each finger if necessary. Weave in ends. ❦

Fair Isle Christmas Stocking

What's better than a gift that holds other gifts? Make one of these extra-special stockings with a snowflake motif for everyone in your family.

Designed by Barb Brown

KNITTED MEASUREMENTS
Length to bottom of heel 13"/33cm
Length from heel to toe 13"/33cm
Width at top 7"/18cm

MATERIALS
■ 1 3½oz/100g skein (each approx 220 yd/201m) of Universal Yarn *Deluxe Worsted* (100% wool) each in #3691 Christmas red (A), #3692 Christmas green (B), and #12257 pulp (C)

■ One set (5) each sizes 4 (3.5mm) and 5 (3.75mm) double-pointed needles (dpns) OR SIZE TO OBTAIN GAUGE

■ Tapestry needle

GAUGE
23 sts and 23 rows = 4"/10cm over chart pat using larger needles.
TAKE TIME TO CHECK GAUGE.

STOCKING
With smaller needles and B, cast on 84 sts. Join to work in the rnd, being careful not to twist, pm at beginning of rnd.

CUFF/LEG
Rnd 1 Purl. Continue in C.
Rnd 2 *K5, sl 1 wyib, rep from * to end.
Rnd 3 *P5, sl 1 wyib, rep from * to end.
Rnds 4 and 5 Repeat rnds 2 and 3.
Rnd 6 Repeat rnd 2.
Rnd 7 Knit.
Rnds 8–10 Work in k1, p1 rib.
Rnd 11 Knit.
Rnd 12 *K1 with C, k1 with A, rep from * to end.
Rnd 13 With A, knit.
With A and C, work 28-st rep of chart 3 times around, through rnd 11 of chart.
Next rnd With A, knit.
Next rnd *K1 with C, k1 with A, rep from * to end.
Next rnd *K1 with B, k1 with C, rep from * to end.
Next rnd With B, knit.
With B and C, work rnds 12–22 of chart, working 28-st rep 3 times around. Work rnds 1–22 once more, and then rnds 1–11 once.
Rearrange stitches as follows for heel: Place first 19 and last 22 sts of rnd onto one needle for heel. Place remaining 43 sts onto holder. Cont with A.

HEEL FLAP (WORKED BACK AND FORTH IN ROWS)
Row 1 (RS) K1, m1, k to end—42 sts.
Row 2 Sl 1, p to end.
Row 3 *Sl 1, k1, rep from * to end.
Row 4 Sl 1, p to end.
Rep rows 3–4 11 times more.

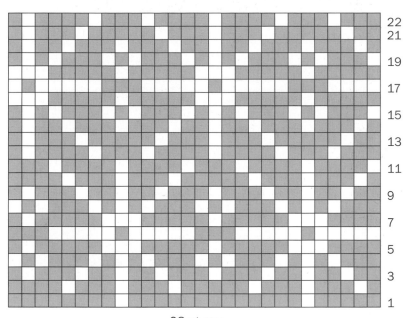

28-st rep

COLOR AND STITCH KEY

☐ (grey) Knit in A or B

☐ (white) Knit in C

TURN HEEL

Row 1 (RS) K21, ssk, k1. Turn.

Row 2(WS) Sl 1, p1, p2tog, p1. Turn.

Row 3 Sl 1, k2, ssk, k1. Turn.

Row 4 Sl 1, p3, p2tog, p1. Turn.

Row 5 Sl 1, k4, ssk, k1. Turn.

Row 6 Sl 1, p5, p2tog, p1. Turn.

Row 7 Sl 1, k6, ssk, k1. Turn.

Row 8 Sl 1, p7, p2tog, p1. Turn.

Row 9 Sl 1, k8, ssk, k1. Turn.

Row 10 Sl 1, p 9, p2tog, p1. Turn.

Row 11 Sl 1, k10, ssk, k1. Turn.

Row 12 Sl 1, p11, p2tog, p1. Turn.

Row 13 Sl 1, k12, ssk, k1. Turn.

Row 14 Sl 1, p13, p2tog, p1. Turn.

Row 15 Sl 1, k14, ssk, k1. Turn.

Row 16 Sl 1, p15, p2tog, p1. Turn.

Row 17 Sl 1, k 16, ssk, k1. Turn.

Row 18 Sl 1, p 17, p2tog, p1. Turn.

Row 19 (RS) Sl 1, k18, ssk, k1. Turn.

Row 20 (WS) Sl 1, p19, p2tog, p1—22 sts. Turn. Cut A.

FOOT

With C, beg working in rnd: Pick up and k 13 sts down right side of heel flap, k across 22 heel sts, pick up and k 13 sts up left side of heel flap. With B and C, work across 43 instep sts, working row 12 of chart as est—89 sts total. Pm to mark beg of sole.

Rnds 1 and 2 Sole: K1 B, k1 C, k2 B, k1 A, *k2 B, k2 A, rep from * 8 times more, k2 B, k1 A, k2 B, k1 A, k1 B, pm to mark end of sole. Instep: Cont to work chart as est with B and C.

Rnd 3 Sole: K1 B, ssk with B, work in stripe pat as est to 3 sts before marker, k2tog with B, k1 B. Instep: Work chart.

Rnd 4 Sole: K2 B, work in stripe pat as est to 2 sts before marker, k2 B. Instep: Work chart.

Rnd 5 Sole: Ssk with B, work in stripe pat as est to 2 sts before marker, k2tog with B. Instep: Work chart.

Rnds 6 and 7 Rep rnds 4 and 5. Cont to work sole in stripe pat as est, and work chart as est for instep, until 88 rnds total of chart have been worked with colors B and C.

Break yarns. Continue in A.

TOE

Rnd 1 Sole: K1, ssk, k to end. Instep: K1, ssk, k to last 3 sts, k2tog, k1—80 sts.

Rnd 2 Knit.

Rnd 3 Sole: K1, ssk, k to last 3 sts, k2tog, k1. Instep: Rep sole.

Rep rnds 2 and 3 until 24 sts rem. Rep rnd 3 only until 12 sts rem. Graft toe using kitchener st.

FINISHING

Weave in all ends.

With RS facing and A, pick up and k 3 sts at top back of stocking.

Row 1 Slide stitches to right end of needle, k3.

Rep row 1 until I-cord measures 6"(15cm). Bind off and attach end to top of stocking in a loop.

Block to measurements. 🎀

Holiday Stranded Wreath

Alternating stripes of different Fair Isle motifs circle this knitted wreath, formed around a foam ring. Hang it all season long to welcome guests.

Designed by Amy Gunderson

KNITTED MEASUREMENTS
Outer circumference 18"/45.5cm

MATERIALS
■ 2 3½oz/100g skeins (each approx 220yd/201m) of Universal Yarn *Deluxe Worsted* (100% wool) in #12501 oatmeal heather (A)

■ 1 skein each in #91475 sangria (B) and #12257 pulp (C)

■ One set (5) size 8 (5mm) double-pointed needles (dpns) OR SIZE TO OBTAIN GAUGE

■ Size H/8 (5mm) crochet hook

■ Waste yarn

■ Tapestry needle

■ 18" Styrofoam wreath form

GAUGE
20 sts and 22 rows = 4"/10cm in color pat using size 8 (5mm) needles.
TAKE TIME TO CHECK GAUGE.

WREATH
With crochet hook and A, ch 60. Beg a few sts from end of chain, pick up and k 48 sts for provisional cast-on. Pm and join to work in the rnd, being careful not to twist. **Work rnds 1–7 of chart 1. With A, knit 1 rnd, and then purl 1 rnd.

SHORT ROW SECTION
Row 1 *With A, k1, with B, k1; rep from * to last st, wrap next st and turn.
Row 2 (WS) *With A, p1, with B, p1; rep from * to 11 sts before beg of rnd (36 sts), wrap next st and turn.
Row 3 *With B, k1, with A, k1; rep from * to 12 sts before last wrapped st (24 sts), wrap next st and turn.
Row 4 *With A, p1, with B, p1; rep from * to 12 sts before last wrapped st (12 sts), wrap next st and turn.
Row 5 *With B, k1, with A, k1; rep from * to end, working wrapped sts tog.
Row 6 With A, knit, working rem wrapped sts tog.
Rnd 7 With A, purl.
Work rnds 1–7 of chart 2. With A, knit 1 rnd. With A, purl 1 rnd.
Rep rows 1–7 of short row section.
Work rnds 1–7 of chart 3. With A, knit 1 rnd. With A, purl 1 rnd.
Rep rows 1–7 of short row section.
Work rnds 1–7 of chart 4. With A, knit 1 rnd. With A, purl 1 rnd.
Rep rows 1–7 of short row section.

Rep from ** 3 times more, then rep from ** once more, omitting last A purl row.
Break yarn, leaving 20"/51cm tail.

FINISHING
Cut wreath form in half. Place both halves into knit wreath.
Carefully remove provisional cast-on and graft cast-on sts tog with live sts from dpns.
Weave in ends. ✄

YARN SNOWMEN

To create snowmen, wrap yarn around foam balls of various sizes. The scarves are knit in stockinette st, and the eyes are the heads of pins. For a carrot nose, wrap orange yarn around a part of a pin or toothpick.

CHART 1

7
5
3
1

8-st rep

CHART 2

7
5
3
1

6-st rep

CHART 3

7
5
3
1

6-st rep

CHART 4

7
5
3
1

6-st rep

COLOR AND STITCH KEY

■ Knit in A

□ Knit in B

Snowlady Hat

Your kids can celebrate a white Christmas by making a snowman—and wearing one! The snowlady on this cute hat has a carrot nose and her own knitted scarf.

◆

Designed by Amy Bahrt

SIZE
Child 2–3 years

KNITTED MEASUREMENTS
Brim circumference approx 17"/43cm

MATERIALS
■ 1 3½oz/100g skein (each approx 220yd/201m) of Universal Yarn *Deluxe Worsted* (100% wool) each in #12177 hot fuschia (A), #12770 natural (B), and #12277 periwinkle (C)

■ Small amount of #12256 tangerine flash

■ One pair each sizes 7 (4.5mm) and 5 (3.75mm) needles
OR SIZE TO OBTAIN GAUGE

■ One set (5) size 7 (4.5mm) double-pointed needles (dpns)

■ Stitch markers

■ Tapestry needle

■ 4" pompom maker

GAUGE
20 sts and 24 rows = 4"/10cm in St st using size 7 (4.5mm) needles.
TAKE TIME TO CHECK GAUGE.

NOTES
1) Hat is worked flat and seamed.
2) Both stranded and intarsia techniques are used to create colorwork.

K1, P1 RIB (MULTIPLE OF 2 STS)
Row 1 *K1, p1, rep from * to end.
Repeat row 1 for k1, p1 rib.

SNOWFLAKE PATTERN
Note Snowflake pattern is stopped at the beginning of the snowlady chart (chart 2) and started again with the beginning of the repeat after the chart.
Row 1 (RS) K3 with C, *k1 with B, k5 with C; rep from * to end.
Row 2 (WS) Purl with C.
Row 3 (RS) Knit with C.
Row 4 (WS) P4 with C, *p3 with C, p1 with B, p2 with C; rep from * to end.
Row 5 (RS) Knit with C.
Row 6 (WS) Purl with C.
Rep rows 1–6 for snowflake pat.

HAT
With smaller needles and A, cast on 86 sts.
Row 1 (RS) Work across in k1, p1 rib.
Change to B.
Rows 2–7 Work across in k1, p1 rib.
Row 8 Purl.
Row 9 Work row 1 from chart 1 in B and C, ending 3 sts B, placing markers after 32nd and 49th sts.
Row 10 (WS) Work row 2 from chart 1 in B and C, ending 2 sts B.

Row 11 K32 with C, work row 1 from chart 2, k to end.
Row 12 Purl to marker, work row 2 from chart 2, purl to end.
Row 13 Work snowflake pat to marker, work chart 2, work snowflake pat to end. Rep row 13 until row 24 of chart 2 is complete, finishing on row 4 of chart 1.
Next row (dec) [K10, k2tog, pm] 7 times, k2.
Next row Purl.

Next row (dec) [K to m, k2tog] 7 times, k2.
Rep last 2 rows until 30 sts rem.
AT SAME TIME, use C for 6 rows, A for 2 rows, C for 2 rows, A for 2 rows, C for two rows, A for rem rows.
Next row Purl.
Next row (dec) K2tog across—15 sts.
Cut yarn, leaving 16"/40cm tail. Weave tail through rem sts, pulling tight. Use tail to seam up hat, using mattress stitch.

FINISHING
Block piece lightly. Weave in ends.

EYES
With strand of C and embroidery needle, form French knots as indicated on chart 2.

CARROT NOSE
With dpns and D, cast on 4 sts and join to work in the rnd, being careful not to twist. Work until piece measures ¾"/2cm. Cut tail and thread through sts, pull tight, and attach other end as indicated on chart.

HAT BRIM
With tapestry needle and A, form chain stitch across bottom of hat, approx 1¼"/3cm, as indicated on chart.

SCARF
With smaller needles and A, cast on 3 sts. Work in St st for 3"/7.5cm. Bind off. With strand of A and tapestry needle, fold and tack at center, extending strand to side around neck.

ARMS
With strand of A and tapestry needle, form chain stitch arms as indicated on chart.

POMPOM
With A, make one 4"/10cm pompom. Attach securely to top of hat using yarn and tapestry needle. 🎀

CHART 1

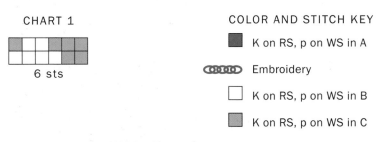

6 sts

COLOR AND STITCH KEY

■ K on RS, p on WS in A

⬤⬤⬤⬤ Embroidery

□ K on RS, p on WS in B

▨ K on RS, p on WS in C

CHART 2

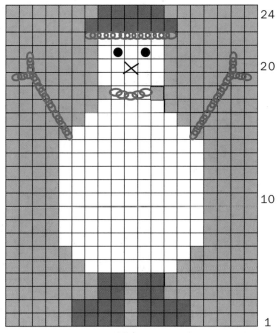

24
20
10
1

19 sts

Christmas Tree Skirt

Crocheted circles on a bright moss stitch background make this skirt such a pretty addition to the tree, you won't want to hide it with presents.

◆

Designed by Laura Maller

KNITTED MEASUREMENTS
Overall diameter approx 42"/107cm
Center diameter approx 7"/18cm

MATERIALS
■ 4 3½oz/100g skeins (each approx 220yd/201m) of Universal Yarn *Deluxe Worsted* (100% wool) in #12279 blue lagoon (A)

■ 1 skein in #3691 Christmas red (B)

■ 2 skeins in #61633 greenery (C)

■ Size 8 (5mm) circular needle, 40"/100cm long, OR SIZE TO OBTAIN GAUGE

■ Size G/6 (4mm) crochet hook

■ Stitch markers

■ Tapestry needle

■ 5 1"/2.5cm buttons

GAUGE
18 stitches and 24 rows = 4"/10cm over double moss stitch using size 8 (5mm) needles.
TAKE TIME TO CHECK GAUGE.

DOUBLE MOSS STITCH
(over odd number of stitches)
Row 1 *K1, p1, rep from * to last st, k1.
Row 2 *P1, k1, rep from * to last st, p1.
Row 3 Rep row 2.
Row 4 Rep row 1.
Repeat rows 1–4 for double moss stitch.

NOTE
Skirt is knit in 7 double moss st sections with a garter st border on each end. The first and last st in each moss section are worked in St st. Increases are worked after the first St st and before the last St st.

TREE SKIRT
With A, cast on 99 sts.
Rows 1–3 Knit.
Row 4 (set-up row) K6, pm, k11, [pm, k13] 5 times, pm, k11, pm, k6.
Row 5 (RS) K6, [k1, work double moss row 1 to 1 st bef m, k1] 7 times, k6.
Row 6 (WS) K6, [p1, work double moss row 2 to 1 st bef m, p1] 7 times, k6.
Row 7 K6, [k1, work double moss row 3 to 1 st bef m, k1] 7 times, k6.
Row 8 K6, [p1, work double moss row 4 to 1 st bef m, p1] 7 times, k6.
Rep rows 5–8 for body of skirt.
Next (inc) row K6, [k1, m1, work double moss until 1 st from marker, m1, k1] 7 times, k6.
Work increases every 2nd row beginning with row 5 ten times; then every 3rd row for remainder.

AT THE SAME TIME, work buttonholes as foll:
On row 5 and every 3½"/9cm after, make a buttonhole on first garter-stitch border:
RS row K2, bind off 3 sts, k1.
WS row K1, cast on 3 sts, k2.
Cont as established until skirt measures 17"/43cm from cast-on edge or desired length, ending with row 8. Knit one row even. Break yarn. Change to B.

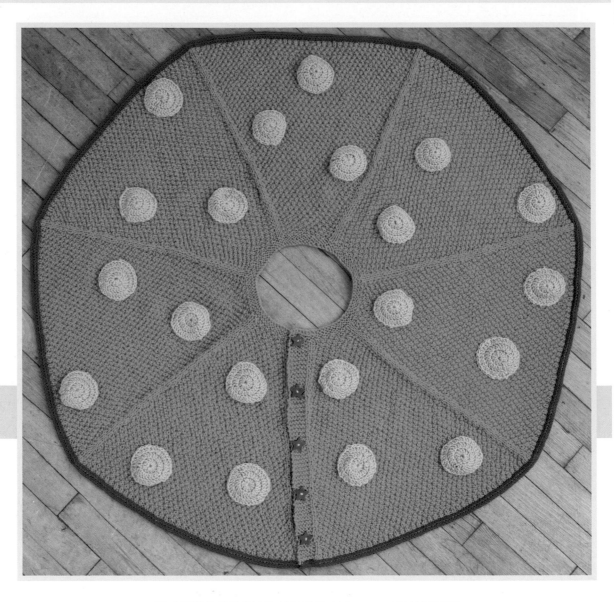

EDGING

Cast on 4 sts.

Row 1 K3, ssk. Put 4 stitches back on left needle as if to purl.

Rep row 1 until all A sts have been knit.

Next row K2tog twice, slip stitches back to left needle, k2tog.

CROCHET CIRCLES (MAKE 21)

With C, ch 3, join with slip st to form ring.

Rnd 1 Ch 3 (counts as first double crochet here and throughout), make 11 dcs in ring, join with slip st to top of ch 3.

Rnd 2 Ch 3, 2 dcs in each stitch around, join with slip st to top of ch 3.

Rnd 3 Ch 3, *2 dcs in next stitch, 1 dc in next stitch, rep from * to last stitch, 2 dcs in last stitch, join with slip st to top of ch 3. Fasten off.

FINISHING

Weave in ends and lightly block. Sew on crochet circles, 3 in each section. Sew buttons opposite buttonholes on garter-stitch edge. 🎀

Decorative Gift Boxes

Arrange these beautifully cabled covers, formed around cardboard boxes, as a holiday centerpiece. Space is left between the cables for a pretty ribbon.

Designed by Rachel Maurer

KNITTED MEASUREMENTS

Large box: 4⅜"/11cm wide x 4⅜"/11cm deep x 5"/13cm tall
Small box: 2⅞"/7.5cm wide x 2⅞"/7.5cm deep x 4"/10cm tall

MATERIALS

■ 2 3½oz/100g skeins (each approx 220yd/201m) of Universal Yarn *Deluxe Worsted* (100% wool) in #12189 baby blue

■ Size 5 (3.75mm) circular needle, 16"/40cm long, OR SIZE TO OBTAIN GAUGE

■ One set (5) size 5 (3.75mm) double-pointed needles (dpns)

■ Cable needle (cn)

■ Stitch markers

■ 2 small tissue boxes

■ 1 pint container, such as for half-and-half, with the top cut off

■ Tapestry needle

■ 3yd/2.7m of ⅝"/1.6cm-wide white grosgrain ribbon

GAUGE

20 stitches and 28 rows = 4"/10cm over St st using size 5 (3.75mm) needle.
TAKE TIME TO CHECK GAUGE.

NOTE

The knitted covers fit very snugly. For ease of finishing, project should be steam blocked and all ends woven in prior to beginning the bottom. The box should be inserted when bottom is two-thirds worked. The remaining rows and finishing can be completed with the insert in place.

STITCH GLOSSARY

cdd (centered double decrease)
Sl 2 sts tog knitwise, k1, psso.
4-st RC Sl 2 sts to cn, hold to *back*, k2, k2 from cn.
4-st LC Sl 2 sts to cn, hold to *front*, k2, k2 from cn.
6-st RC Sl 3 sts to cn, hold to *back*, k3, k3 from cn.
6-st LC Sl 3 sts to cn, hold to *front*, k3, k3 from cn.
4-st RPC Sl 2 sts to cn, hold to *back*, k2, p2 from cn.
4-st LPC Sl 2 sts to cn, hold to *front*, p2, k2 from cn.
4-st RCS Sl 2 sts to cn, hold to *back*, k2, [p1, k1] from cn.
4-st LCS Sl 2 sts to cn, hold to *front*, k2, p1, k2 from cn.

LARGE BOXES (MAKE 2)
SIDES

With circular needle, cast on 100 sts. Join to work in the rnd, being careful not to twist, place marker (pm) at beg of rnd.
Rnds 1–37 *Follow charts 1 and 2 (for 2nd box, charts 1 and 3), rep from * once more for rnd.

145

TOP

Rnd 1 Knit.

Rnd 2 K24, cdd, [k22, cdd] three times—move round marker to after final cdd on this and every rnd.

Rnd 3 K21, cdd, [k20, cdd] 3 times.

Rnd 4 K19, cdd, [k18, cdd] 3 times.

Rnd 5 K17, cdd, [k16, cdd] 3 times.

Rnd 6 K15, cdd, [k14, cdd] 3 times.

Rnd 7 K13, cdd, [k12, cdd] 3 times.

Rnd 8 K11, cdd, [k10, cdd] 3 times.

Rnd 9 K9, cdd, [k8, cdd] 3 times.

Rnd 10 K7, cdd, [k6, cdd] 3 times.

Rnd 11 K5, cdd, [k4, cdd] 3 times.

Rnd 12 K3, cdd, [k2, cdd] 3 times.

Rnd 13 [Cdd] 4 times.

Cut yarn and thread through stitches, pulling tight. Secure.

BOTTOM

With RS facing, pick up and k 18 sts on side B, 25 sts on side A, and 18 sts on side D. Cut yarn.

With WS facing, sl 19 sts, pass the 18th st slipped over the 19th and move back to left needle.

Row 1 P24, sl second st on left needle over the first, p1, turn.

Row 2 K24, sl second st on left needle over first, k1, turn.

Rep rows 1 and 2 18 times, until all side sts are used. Bind off.

FINISHING

Using mattress stitch, seam together bottom and side panels. Weave in any remaining ends. 🪰

SMALL BOX
SIDES

With dpns, cast on 64 sts. Join in the round, being careful not to twist, pm at beg of round.

Rnds 1–30 Follow chart 4, rep each row of chart 4 times for rnd.

TOP

Rnd 1 Knit.

Rnd 2 K15, cdd [k13, cdd] 3 times—move round marker to after final cdd on this and every rnd.

Rnd 3 K12, cdd, [k11, cdd] 3 times.

Rnd 4 K10, cdd, [k9, cdd] 3 times.

Rnd 5 K8, cdd, [k7, cdd] 3 times.

Rnd 6 K6, cdd, [k5, cdd] 3 times.

Rnd 7 K4, cdd, [k3, cdd] 3 times.

Rnd 8 [Cdd, k1] twice.

Cut yarn and thread through stitches, pulling tight. Secure.

BOTTOM

With RS facing, pick up and k 12 sts on side B, 16 sts on side A, and 12 sts on side D. Cut yarn.

With WS facing, sl 13 sts, pass the 12th st slipped over the 13th and move back to left needle.

Row 1 P24, sl second st on left needle over the first, p1, turn.

Row 2 K24, sl second st on left needle over first, k1, turn.

Rep rows 1 and 2 twelve times, until all side sts are used. Bind off.

FINISHING

Using mattress stitch, seam together bottom and side panels. Weave in any remaining ends. 🪰

CHART 1

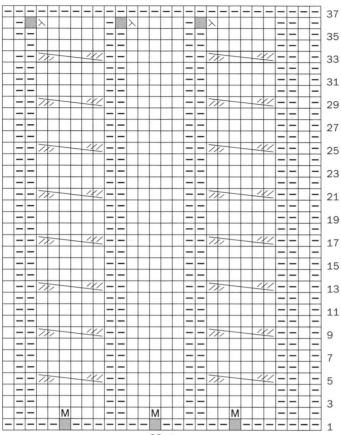

28 sts

CHART 2

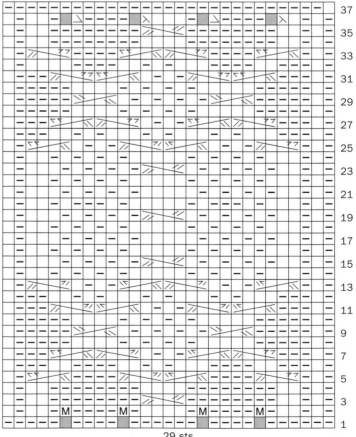

29 sts

148

CHART 3

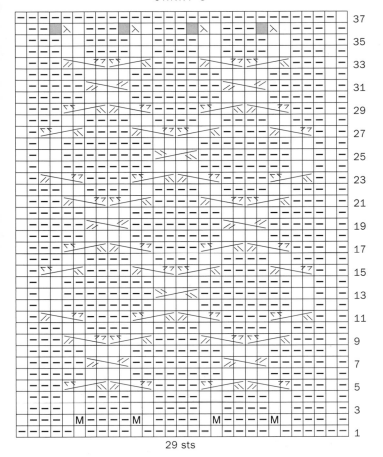

29 sts

CHART 4

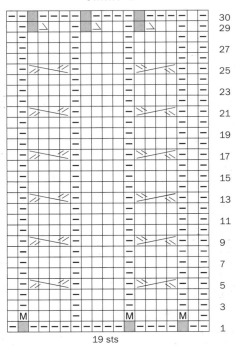

19 sts

STITCH KEY

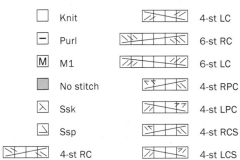

☐	Knit	
–	Purl	
M	M1	
▨	No stitch	
⊼	Ssk	
⊿	Ssp	
	4-st RC	

	4-st LC
	6-st RC
	6-st LC
	4-st RPC
	4-st LPC
	4-st RCS
	4-st LCS

Helpful Information

Knitting Needles

U.S.	METRIC
0	2mm
1	2.25mm
2	2.75mm
3	3.25mm
4	3.5mm
5	3.75mm
6	4mm
7	4.5mm
8	5mm
9	5.5mm
10	6mm
10½	6.5mm
11	8mm
13	9mm
15	10mm
17	12.75mm
19	15mm
35	19mm

Abbreviations

approx approximately
beg begin(ning)
CC contrasting color
ch chain
cm centimeter(s)
cn cable needle
cont continu(e)(ing)
dec decreas(e)(ing)
dpn double-pointed needle(s)
foll follow(s)(ing)
g gram(s)
inc increas(e)(ing)
k knit
k2tog knit 2 sts tog (one st has been decreased)
LH left-hand
lp(s) loop(s)
m meter(s)
mm millimeter(s)
MC main color
M1 make one st; with needle tip, lift strand between last st knit and next st on LH needle and knit into back of it
M1 p-st make 1 purl st
oz ounce(s)
p purl

pat(s) pattern(s)
pm place marker
psso pass slip stitch(es) over
rem remain(s)(ing)
rep repeat
RH right-hand
RS right side(s)
rnd(s) round(s)
SKP slip 1, knit 1, pass slip st over (one st has been decreased)
SK2P slip 1, knit 2 tog, pass slip st over the knit 2 tog (two sts have been decreased)
S2KP slip 2 sts tog, knit 1, pass 2 slip sts over knit 1 (two sts have been decreased)
sl slip
sl st slip stitch
ssk slip 2 sts kwise, one at a time; insert tip of LH needle into front of these sts and knit them tog (one st has been decreased)

ssp slip 2 sts kwise, one at a time, wyif, insert tip of LH needle into back of these sts and knit them tog (one stitch has been decreased)
sssk slip 3 sts kwise, one at a time; insert tip of LH needle into front of these sts and knit them tog (two sts have been decreased)
st(s) stitch(es)
St st stockinette stitch
tbl through back loop(s)
tog together
WS wrong side(s)
wyib with yarn in back
wyif with yarn in front
yd yard(s)
yo yarn over needle
* repeat directions following *
[ ] repeat directions inside brackets as many times as indicated

Glossary

as foll Work the instructions that follow.

bind off Used to finish an edge or segment. Lift the first stitch over the second, the second over the third, etc. (U.K.: cast off)

bind off in ribbing Work in ribbing as you bind off. (Knit the knit stitches, purl the purl stitches.) (U.K.: cast off in ribbing)

3-needle bind-off With the right side of the two pieces facing and the needles parallel, insert a third needle into the first stitch on each needle and knit them together. Knit the next two stitches the same way. Slip the first stitch on the third needle over the second stitch and off the needle. Repeat for three-needle bind-off.

cast on Placing a foundation row of stitches upon the needle in order to begin knitting

decrease Reduce the stitches in a row (that is, knit 2 together).

hold to front (back) of work Usually refers to stitches placed on a cable needle that are held to the front (or back) of the work as it faces you.

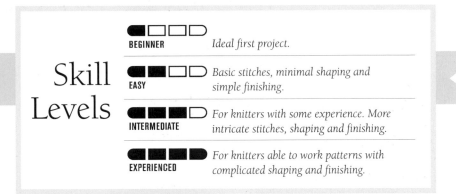

BEGINNER		*Ideal first project.*
EASY		*Basic stitches, minimal shaping and simple finishing.*
INTERMEDIATE		*For knitters with some experience. More intricate stitches, shaping and finishing.*
EXPERIENCED		*For knitters able to work patterns with complicated shaping and finishing.*

Skill Levels

increase Add stitches in a row (that is, knit in front and back of stitch).

knitwise Insert the needle into the stitch as if you were going to knit it.

make one With the needle tip, lift the strand between the last stitch knit and the next stitch on the left-hand needle and knit into back of it. One knit stitch has been added.

make one p-st With the needle tip, lift the strand between the last stitch worked and the next stitch on the left-hand needle and purl it. One purl stitch has been added.

no stitch On some charts, "no stitch" is indicated with shaded spaces where stitches have been decreased or not yet made. In such cases, work the stitches of the chart, skipping over the "no stitch" spaces.

place markers Place or attach a loop of contrast yarn or purchased stitch marker as indicated.

pick up and knit (purl) Knit (or purl) into the loops along an edge.

purlwise Insert the needle into the stitch as if you were going to purl it.

selvedge stitch Edge stitch that helps make seaming easier.

slip, slip, knit Slip next two stitches knitwise, one at a time, to right-hand needle. Insert tip of left-hand needle into fronts of these stitches, from left to right. Knit them together. One stitch has been decreased.

slip, slip, slip, knit Slip next three stitches knitwise, one at a time, to right-hand needle. Insert tip of left-hand needle into fronts of these stitches, from left to right. Knit them together. Two stitches have been decreased.

slip stitch An unworked stitch made by passing a stitch from the left-hand to the right-hand needle as if to purl.

stockinette stitch Knit every right-side row and purl every wrong-side row.

work even Continue in pattern without increasing or decreasing. (U.K.: work straight)

work to end Work the established pattern to the end of the row.

Useful Techniques

CABLES

Note: Cables shown are 6-stitch cables (3 sts on each side). Twists are made with 2 stitches (1 on each side). Stitch glossaries in each pattern specify stitch counts for cables used in that pattern.

FRONT (OR LEFT) CABLE

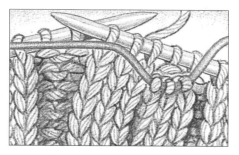

1. Slip the first 3 stitches of the cable purlwise to a cable needle and hold them to the front of the work. Be careful not to twist the stitches.

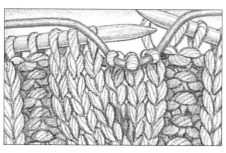

2. Leave the stitches suspended in front of the work, keeping them in the center of the cable needle where they won't slip off. Pull the yarn firmly and knit the next 3 stitches.

3. Knit the 3 stitches from the cable needle. If this seems too awkward, return the stitches to the left needle and then knit them. ✻

BACK (OR RIGHT) CABLE

1. Slip the first 3 stitches of the cable purlwise to a cable needle and hold them to the back of the work. Be careful not to twist the stitches.

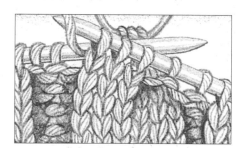

2. Leave the stitches suspended in back of the work, keeping them in the center of the cable needle where they won't slip off. Pull the yarn firmly and knit the next 3 stitches.

3. Knit the 3 stitches from the cable needle. If this seems too awkward, return the stitches to the left needle and then knit them. ✻

YARN OVERS

A yarn over is a decorative increase made by wrapping the yarn around the needle. There are various ways to make a yarn over depending on where it is placed.

BETWEEN TWO KNIT STITCHES
Bring the yarn from the back of the work to the front between the two needles. Knit the next stitch, bringing the yarn to the back over the right needle as shown. 🐝

BETWEEN A KNIT AND A PURL STITCH Bring the yarn from the back to the front between the two needles, then to the back over the right needle and to the front again as shown. Purl the next stitch. 🐝

BETWEEN A PURL AND A KNIT STITCH Leave the yarn at the front of the work. Knit the next stitch, bringing the yarn to the back over the right needle as shown. 🐝

BETWEEN TWO PURL STITCHES
Leave the yarn at the front of the work. Bring the yarn to the back over the right needle and to the front again as shown. Purl the next stitch. 🐝

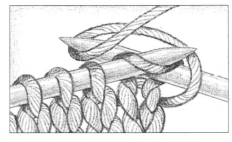

AT THE BEGINNING OF A KNIT ROW Keep the yarn at the front of the work. Insert the right needle knitwise into the first stitch on the left needle. Bring the yarn over the right needle to the back and knit the next stitch, holding the yarn over with your thumb if necessary. 🐝

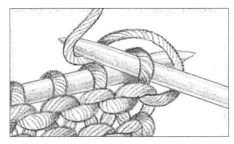

AT THE BEGINNING OF A PURL ROW To work a yarn over at the beginning of a purl row, keep the yarn at the back of the work. Insert the right needle purlwise into the first stitch on the left needle. Purl the stitch. 🐝

MULTIPLE YARN OVERS
1. For multiple yarn overs (two or more), wrap the yarn around the needle as for a single yarn over, then wrap the yarn around the needle once more (or as many times as indicated). Work the next stitch on the left needle.

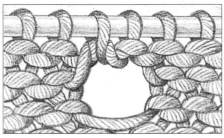

2. Alternate knitting and purling into the multiple yarn over on the subsequent row, always knitting the last stitch on a purl row and purling the last stitch on a knit row. 🐝

PICKING UP STITCHES

ALONG A HORIZONTAL EDGE

1. Insert the knitting needle into the center of the first stitch in the row below the bound-off edge. Wrap the yarn knitwise around the needle.

ALONG A VERTICAL EDGE

1. Insert the knitting needle into the corner stitch of the first row, one stitch in from the side edge. Wrap the yarn around the needle knitwise.

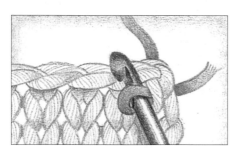

WITH A CROCHET HOOK

1. Insert the crochet hook from front to back into the center of the first stitch one row below the bound-off edge. Catch the yarn and pull a loop through.

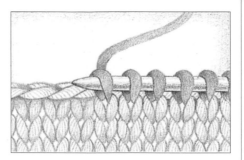

2. Draw the yarn through. You have picked up one stitch. Continue to pick up one stitch in each stitch along the bound-off edge. 🐝

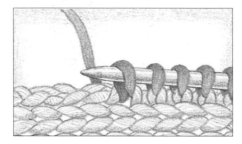

2. Draw the yarn through. You have picked up one stitch. Continue to pick up stitches along the edge. Occasionally skip one row to keep the edge from flaring. 🐝

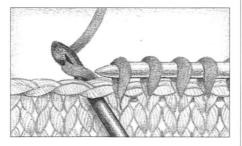

2. Slip the loop onto the knitting needle, being sure it is not twisted. Continue to pick up one stitch in each stitch along the bound-off edge. 🐝

◆ CROCHETED CHAIN

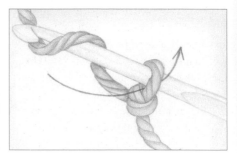

1. Make a slipknot and place it on the hook. Draw the yarn through the loop on the hook by catching it with the hook and pulling it toward you.

2. One chain stitch is complete. Lightly tug on the yarn to tighten the loop if it is very loose, or wiggle the hook to loosen the loop if it is tight. Repeat from step 1 to make as many chain stitches as required for your pattern. 🐝

HOW TO MAKE A POMPOM

1. With two circular pieces of cardboard the width of the desired pompom, cut a center hole. Then cut a pie-shaped wedge out of the circle. (Use the picture as a guide.)

2. Tightly hold the two circles together and wrap the yarn tightly around the cardboard. Then carefully cut around the cardboard.

3. Tie a piece of yarn tightly between the two circles. Remove the cardboard and trim the pompom.

4. Sandwich pompom between two round pieces of cardboard held together with a long needle. Cut around the circumference for a perfect pompom.

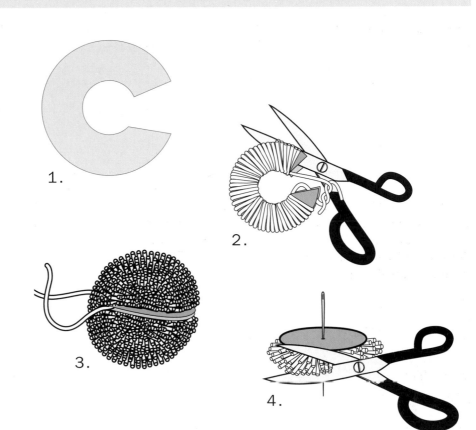

1.

2.

3.

4.

EMBROIDERY STITCHES

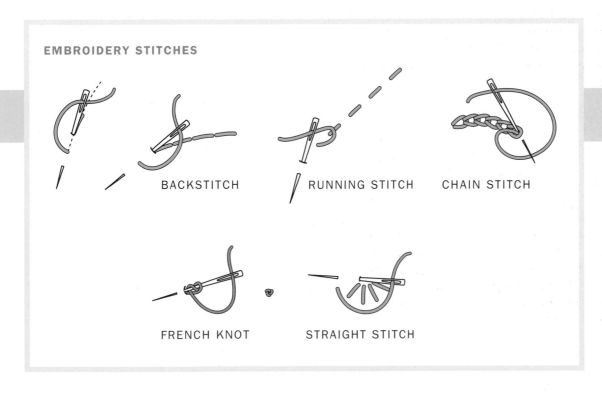

BACKSTITCH   RUNNING STITCH   CHAIN STITCH

FRENCH KNOT   STRAIGHT STITCH

About the Yarns

FABRIC CARE AND BLOCKING

Maintain the beauty and lasting warmth of projects made in Universal Yarn Deluxe Worsted (100% wool) (**4**) by following proper care guidelines. Hand wash all finished projects by submerging them in cold water with a small amount of gentle soap. Carefully wash the garment, being careful not to create too much friction, and rinse in cold water. Gently remove excess water and dry finished garments flat or on a blocking board. It is not recommended that bleach or an iron be used on the yarn or fabric.

WHERE TO FIND UNIVERSAL YARN DELUXE WORSTED

Visit the Universal Yarn website at www.UniversalYarn.com to see the full collection of colors and textures in the Deluxe Collection of wools, and to find a U.S.-based Deluxe Worsted retailer near you.

**UNIVERSAL YARN
(IN THE U.S.)**
5991 Caldwell Park Drive
Harrisburg, NC 28075
Tel: 877.864.9276
Fax: 704.454.1559
e-mail: patterns@universalyarn.com
www.universalyarn.com

CANADA
Diamond Yarn
155 Martin Ross Ave Unit 3
Toronto (Ont.) M3J2L9
Tel: 800.268.1896
Fax: 416.736.6112
www.diamondyarn.com

MEXICO
Rebecca Pick Estambres
Lago Chalco No. 129 Col Anahuac
C.P. 1320 Mexico, D.F.
Tel: 52.5341.4413
Fax: 52.5341.6019
www.rebeccapickestambres.com

TURKEY
Defne
Yeni Yalova Yolu Buttim Plaza
Kat. 19 No: 1663/Bursa
Tel: 90.224.221.0750
Fax: 90.224.211.0753
e-mail: info@defneiplikpazarlama.com

Standard Yarn Weight System

Categories of yarn, gauge ranges, and recommended needle and hook sizes

Yarn Weight Symbol & Category Names	0 Lace	1 Super Fine	2 Fine	3 Light	4 Medium	5 Bulky	6 Super Bulky
Type of Yarns in Category	Fingering 10 count crochet thread	Sock, Fingering, Baby	Sport, Baby	DK, Light Worsted	Worsted, Afghan, Aran	Chunky, Craft, Rug	Bulky, Roving
Knit Gauge Range* in Stockinette Stitch to 4 inches	33–40** sts	27–32 sts	23–26 sts	21–24 sts	16–20 sts	12–15 sts	6–11 sts
Recommended Needle in Metric Size Range	1.5–2.25 mm	2.25–3.25 mm	3.25–3.75 mm	3.75–4.5 mm	4.5–5.5 mm	5.5–8 mm	8 mm and larger
Recommended Needle U.S. Size Range	000 to 1	1 to 3	3 to 5	5 to 7	7 to 9	9 to 11	11 and larger
Crochet Gauge* Ranges in Single Crochet to 4 inch	32-42 double crochets**	21–32 sts	16–20 sts	12–17 sts	11–14 sts	8–11 sts	5–9 sts
Recommended Hook in Metric Size Range	Steel*** 1.6–1.4mm Regular hook 2.25 mm	2.25–3.5 mm	3.5–4.5 mm	4.5–5.5 mm	5.5–6.5 mm	6.5–9 mm	9 mm and larger
Recommended Hook U.S. Size Range	Steel*** 6, 7, 8 Regular hook B–1	B–1 to E–4	E–4 to 7	7 to I–9	I–9 to K–10½	K–10½ to M–13	M–13 and larger

* GUIDELINES ONLY: The above reflect the most commonly used gauges and needle or hook sizes for specific yarn categories.

** Lace weight yarns are usually knitted or crocheted on larger needles and hooks to create lacy, openwork patterns. Accordingly, a gauge range is difficult to determine. Always follow the gauge stated in your pattern.

*** Steel crochet hooks are sized differently from regular hooks--the higher the number, the smaller the hook, which is the reverse of regular hook sizing.

This Standards & Guidelines booklet and downloadable symbol artwork are available at: **YarnStandards.com**

Knitted Gifts Planning Guide

This is a general guide to how long the projects in this book take to knit. While these time frames do take a project's finishing requirements (including felting) into account, they don't include its prep time (gathering the yarn and other supplies, knitting and blocking a gauge swatch, and so on). Because everyone knits at his or her own rate of speed, it's best to err on the side of caution and plan for the far end of a time frame, especially if you're a beginner or like to knit at a relaxed pace.

Contributing Designers

Index